ONE GEAR

*Converting and maintaining
single speed & fixed gear bicycles*

Design by Luca Bendandi
Texts by Matteo Cossu, unless otherwise credited.

Photography by Luca Gambi, unless otherwise stated.
Photoediting by Ruben Cruz
Proofreading by John Z. Komurki

Published in 2011 by
Gingko Press Inc.
1321 Fifth Street
Berkeley, CA 94710, USA
Ph: (510) 898 -1195
Em: books@gingkopress.com
www.gingkopress.com

ISBN: 978-1-58423-418-0
LCCN: 2011928512

First Edition

Table of Contents

**Cranksets, anodized aluminum
and an eagle-eye for details.**

On the Beauty of Bikes

A bicycle can be many things. Most of all, and for most of us, it's an efficient, clean and inexpensive means of transportation. But, as for many things that have arisen from function, people's passion has turned it into an object revered for its form. Fixed-gear bikes were the first kind of bikes to appear, and were then adapted for oval track racing, where they were merely a tool to achieve maximum speed. From these pure competitive origins, the fixed-gear took to the streets, carrying an almost inexplicable charm.

An elemental bike, stripped of all nonessential elements – no brakes, no gears, no cables. A diamond frame, two wheels, pedals and a chain. And if we are looking to define the fixed-gear allure then we can begin here: a fixed-gear bike is the purest kind of bicycle there is. Around the fixie – as it is affectionately called – the scene has grown, propelled by track racers turned bike messengers, hill bombers, tricksters and bike aesthetic junkies. A fixie is, more often than not, a beautiful and very personal item.

We believe that being the proud creator of a beautiful ride is one of the most rewarding challenges a bike lover can tackle. This book sets out to explore the best way of giving an old road bike a new life. Customization is at the heart of this endeavor, and expertise comes with experience and practice. Train your eye for details: because amongst fixed-gear riders discussions about chain-line, cog options and hubs are almost as popular as riding their bikes.

The right bike

Shopping for a vintage road bike is a tricky, but potentially rewarding task. A road bike is a fairly common object; apart from bike shops, other possible treasure troves include pawnshops, garage sales and second-hand stores. When looking for a project bike in one of these places, keep your eyes open for a gem hidden under thirty or fourty years of dust and grime.

This chapter will give you details how to spot a diamond in the rough: how to tell a quality vintage bike from a cheaper model, and what characteristics to look for ease of conversion. Bike purchase stories are like fish stories, the "catch" only seems to get bigger and better. You may hear of the occasional gem found in a friend's attic, but more often than not sellers will know what they have on their hands.

That is not to say that you can't get good deals: most people prefer buying a newer, inferior quality bike instead of dedicating hours of work restoring an older better built frameset. In conclusion, vintage bike shopping isn't just a matter of budget. Armed with a little luck, knowledge, and an idea of the time and work involved in your conversion you'll have an extremely satisfying first ride.

Above Below, Andy Miller

Frame, Gaëtan Rossier
www.gaetanrossier.ch

First Impressions Count

What characteristics to look for in a bike you plan to convert

a) Size
You should always try out the bike to see how it feels. If that's not an option, compare sizes (see table on page 17) and pick accordingly. Remember that an under or oversized frame won't do.

b) Dropouts
Most vintage bikes have horizontal dropouts which are optimal for singlespeed conversions.

c) Crankset
Look for a three piece crankset, so you'll be able to get rid of extra chainrings if necessary. Cottered cranks (held on by pins) are usually hard to remove and reinstall, so try to avoid them.

d) Hubs
If you're looking to keep the back wheel, look for a bike that has older thread-on (freewheel) hubs.

e) Frame tubing
Ideally you'll want something built by a good tube manufacturer, for both lightness and longevity. Welded frames (as per the example at left) are great, but don't be afraid of good old lugs.

f) Components
Brand-name components are pricier, but they make for an overall higher-quality bike.

g) Pedals
Higher quality pedals will already be fitted with cages or suited for toe straps.

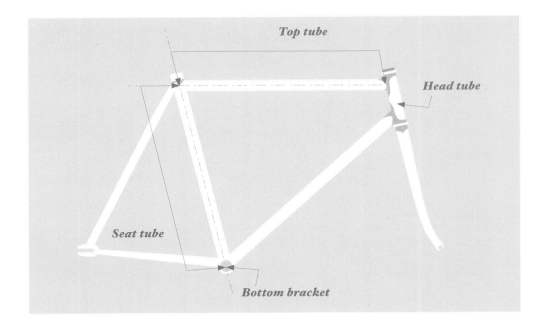

Geometry

Modern (post-1990) road bike geometry tends to be fairly different from that of older, vintage bikes. The top tube is sloped at an angle towards the seat. The rear end of the bike is also very short, so that the rear wheel can rest closer to the seat tube.

A vintage road bike has a distinct look: it has a longer top horizontal tube, which hangs parallel to the ground, and the chainstays (the back of the bike) are longer, allowing the wheel to rest further away from the seat tube.

Size

In case you find only one measure defining frame size, it generally refers to the length of the seat tube. When shopping for a vintage road bike, one can't be too picky, and a general rule of thumb is that you should be able to stand over it comfortably. However, it can't be too short, otherwise you'll be forced to raise the saddle too high to extend your legs properly and handlebars will end up too low, creating an uncomfortable riding position.

Another rule of thumb is that you should ride the largest bike which you are able to stand comfortably over.

Measurement

Over the years manufacturers have come up with disparate ways of measuring tubes, but we'll stick to the commonest. The seat tube should be measured from the center of the crank to the center of the top tube.

Top tube (horizontal tube)

A lot of vintage road bikes have short top tubes. A good way to see if the top tube's long enough is to place your elbow on the end of the saddle, extending your arm to the stem. For optimal comfort your fingers shouldn't extend over the handlebars.

Seat angle

There are different philosophies regarding this, but the seat should always be tested for comfort. A good starting point is absolutely level, parallel to the ground. In any case, most saddle stays are widely customizable.

Your Height		Seat Tube	
cm	ft	cm	in
150	4' 11"	46 - 47	18.1-18.5
155	5' 1"	48 - 49	18.9-19.3
160	5' 3"	50 - 51	19.7-20
165	5' 5"	52 - 53	20.5-20.9
170	5' 7"	54 - 55	21.2-21.6
175	5' 9"	56 - 57	22-22.4
180	5' 11"	58 - 59	22.8-23.2
185	6' 1"	60 - 61	23.6-24
190	6' 3"	62 -63	24.4-24.8

Dropouts

The dropout is the part of the bike where the rear-wheel bolts to the frame. Dropouts are the most important feature to look at when shopping for a good vintage roadbike to convert. When the derailleur–the system which shifts gears on a road bike–is removed, then the chain must be tensioned by moving the wheel back or forth. That can be accomplished easily on roadbikes with horizontal dropouts *(a,b,c,d)*.

There are ways to convert a frame with vertical or semi-vertical dropouts, but this requires expensive extra parts. Vertical dropouts *(e,f)* have a vertical notch for the axle to go up into, and the axle's position is not adjustable. With vertical dropouts, the axle cannot be pulled out of position, even if it is not properly secured.

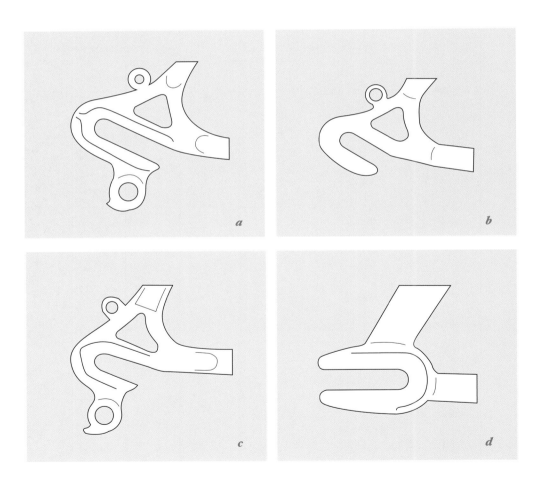

a

b

c

d

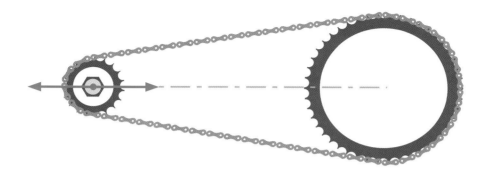

a,b,c) Horizontal dropouts

This is the easiest type of dropout to convert to a single-speed, and luckily they are found on most older road bikes.

d) Track fork ends

Not exactly a dropout but a forged end. They are usually found on track bikes and on older one-speed cruiser bikes.

e) Semi-vertical dropouts

These dropouts have a slight adjustment margin, but you will usually need to resort to destructive techniques such as filing to get more space.

f) Vertical dropouts

Completely vertical dropouts will be found on more modern roadbikes. Without special eccentric hubs it's practically impossible to reach satisfactory chain tension.

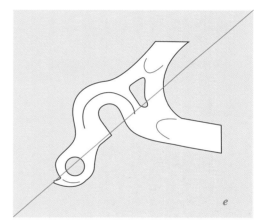

e

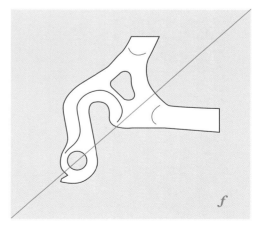

f

Drive Train

Drive train types are also an important consideration. Bikes with shorter crank arms and three-piece cranks (*a*) are better candidates. Shorter cranks (165 -170mm) have higher ground clearance which is important in a fixed-gear bike conversion.
Cheaper quality cranks are swaged together with the spider or chainwheel (*b*). In better cranksets, the right crank and the spider are one forge, making them straighter and more durable. Three piece cranks also give you the option of changing the chainring.

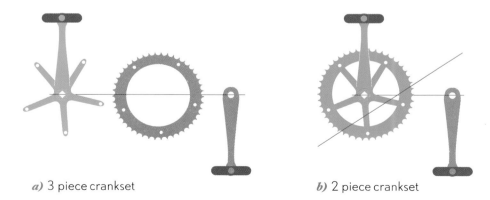

a) 3 piece crankset   *b)* 2 piece crankset

Bottom Brackets

The bottom bracket connects both cranks and allows them to rotate freely. On the inside, it houses a spindle to which the crankset is attached. The bearings run around the spindle allowing it and the cranks to rotate.

French bottom brackets

Older French bikes will have right-threaded bottom brackets which tend to unscrew during use. This makes it impossible to adapt other bottom bracket types, but any good bike shop will carry a tap to convert the threading.

 French bottom bracket: counter clockwise threading

 Common bottom bracket: clockwise threading

Unfortunately it isn't easy to tell the difference between a French bottom bracket and an ISO English type by eye, but if you suspect that the bike was made in France it is wise to ask the seller for clarification. Of course, It's possible to use an apposite bottom bracket tap to convert French to English threading, but it's a job for a bike shop and will increase the overall cost of your conversion

Rear hubs

Most fixed gear conversions are done by replacing the rear wheel, and this is generally the safest, best way to go. It does, however, involve buying a new wheel so this isn't the cheapest option. Modern bikes have a cassette hub or a free-hub. Check the table below.

	Conversion to Fixed-gear	*Conversion to Singlespeed freewheel*
Cassette hub	Surly Fixxer® Cassette hub converter expensive	Slide-on freewheel cog with spacers. cheap
Freewheel hub	Screw-on fixed cog, secured with glue or the Pettenella method. cheap	Screw-on freewheel cog with spacers. cheap

Cassette hub / free-hub

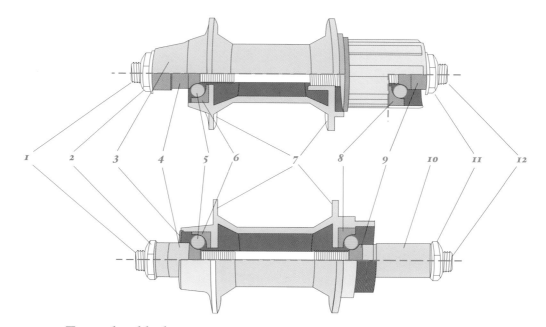

Freewheel hub

1. Axle *2.* Locknut *3.* Dust cover *4.* Bearing cone *5.* Ball bearing
6. Bearing cup *7.* Flanges with spoke holes *8.* Bearing Cup *9.* Bearing cone
10. Spacer *11.* Lock nut *12.* Axle

Frame Tubing

Modern bicycles are increasingly made of carbon fiber, aluminum, or titanium but most vintage road bikes (pre 1990) are made of steel.
There are various qualities of steel tubing, but better steel alloys–usually employed on higher-end bikes–allow for thinner tubes, minimizing the overall weight of the frame. Usually there are decals that indicate the quality of the steel. References to **4130**, **chromoly steel** or **Cr-Mo** are the better choice. If, on the other hand, there are references to **1020, hi-resilience, hi-ten** or similar, it's a sign of a poorer quality steel.
There are various tube manufacturers, such as **Columbus, Reynolds, Tange, Vitus,** and usually these bikes are made with better quality steel.

 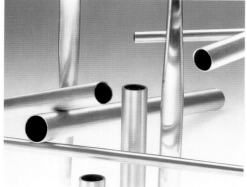

Columbus is probably the best-known tubing manufacturer in the bike business. Mr. Colombo himself started the business back in the 1930's. In 1931, the company was building welded and seamless steel tubes for bicycles and motorcycles (Moto Guzzi was winning with frames made of Colombus tubes), cars, and airplanes. His first customers were mostly small manufacturers but also leading cycling factories: Edoardo Bianchi, Umberto Dei, Atala, Giovanni Maino, and the Doniselli brothers. A Columbus tubing sticker on a bike is always a guarantee of a quality frame. Even their lower-end tubing is made with a standard of quality rarely found in other brands.

If the sticker's missing, you can recognize a Columbus frame by the fact that the outer surface of the fork steerer tube will probably have the Columbus logo (a little dove). Another way to tell is if the lower portion of the inside of the steerer has ridges. If you find either of these clues, the fork tubing is almost certainly Columbus–and if the fork is original, so is everything else. Nevertheless, if either the dove or the ridges are missing, it may still be a Columbus frame.

Photo courtesy of Archivio Columbus

Photo by Luca Bendandi
ihardlyknowher.com/brembo

How to Fit a Bicycle

by *Peter Jon White*
of Peter White Cycles, Hillsborough, NH, USA
www.peterwhitecycles.com

Overview

Bicycle fitting is a subject most people find quite mysterious. Fitting systems with charts and graphs, computer software, measuring devices and "rules of thumb" make for a lot of confusion. But it's really quite simple. Bicycle fitting involves compromises: compromises between comfort and performance, quick acceleration and handling stability, top speed and "taking in the scenery". Your body's position on the bike affects how you ride. It affects how much power you can efficiently deliver to the pedals. It affects how comfortable you are on the bike. A position that is more comfortable may not allow you to put as much energy into moving the bike forward as a less comfortable position. So how do you decide where to position your body on the bike?

Question: where do you ride and for how long?

A track sprinter is not the least bit concerned with how comfortable he is sitting on the bike. During the race (which may last for less than a minute) he may only be seated for 5 or 10 seconds. A long distance tourist traveling coast-to-coast across the USA might spend 5 to 12 hours a day in the saddle, day after day. He is probably far more concerned with being comfortable and enjoying the scenery than with going as fast as he can.

Some considerations to start with

Your body is in contact with the bicycle in three areas; your hands, your seat, and your feet. The relative positions of feet, seat and hands determine your comfort and efficiency on the bike. There are several variables that determine these positions: crank length, distance from crank center (or bottom bracket) to saddle, saddle angle, seat tube angle and saddle offset, distance from saddle to handlebar, relative height of saddle and handlebar, handlebar width, and handlebar drop on road style handlebars. Let's look at each of these variables.

Crank length determines the diameter of the circle that the pedals move in. The larger that circle is, the more flexion of your knee and thigh muscles will be needed to turn the cranks. Your thigh muscles cannot exert the same force throughout their range of motion. This is very easy to demonstrate. If you squat down so that your knees are fully bent and lift yourself up, say, 13 cm (5 in), it takes a good deal more effort than it would to squat down just 13 cm (5 in) from standing straight and then lift yourself back up. In other words, in the full squat position, your muscles can't put out the same power as when your knees are just bent enough to drop you down five inches. So if you had to choose between a crank length that had your knees bending through their entire range of motion and a length that only required, say, 20 degrees of flexion at the knee, you would choose the shorter crank. That crank would have your muscles working through a more efficient range of motion. You would thus avoid forcing your knees to work as hard in an inefficient manner.

So how long should the cranks be? Some research has been done to determine the optimum percentage of leg length to crank length. There isn't a standard value, but a percentage of 18.5% of the distance from the top of the femur to the floor (in bare feet) should be the crank length. You can find the top of the femur pretty easily. It's 12 to 15 cm below your hipbone, and moves backwards when you raise your knee. So, in theory, 175 mm cranks are usually a better fit to an average height rider. However, in the case of fixed-gear bikes, shorter cranks should be chosen to allow for clearance of obstacles, since it is impossible to coast over an obstacle.

Saddle height

Once the crank length is determined (by whatever means), the saddle should be set at a nominal height. There is no objectively determined ideal saddle height for any rider based on leg length alone. Some riders naturally pedal toes down, while others have the foot in a more level position. For starters, sit on the saddle with one leg hanging free and your hips square (not tilting to either side). Set the saddle high enough that your other heel can just touch the pedal with your leg straight, and with the pedal at the bottom of the stroke, in line with the seat tube. For most people this results in a saddle height that leaves some bend in the knee at the bottom of the pedal stroke, when pedaling with the balls of the feet over the axle of the pedals. It also should prevent you from having to rock your hips through each crank rotation. This gets you close enough to your optimum saddle height that you can go through the rest of the fitting process and fine-tune saddle height later. Any later saddle height adjustments shouldn't be large enough to throw off the other adjustments, with the exception of handlebar height, which is easily changed.

The fore-aft saddle position

Now we get to what I think is the most important part of fitting a bicycle, the fore-aft position of the saddle. Once you get this right, everything else is easy. This position is determined more by how you intend to use your bike than by anything else. If you look at a typical bike, the saddle is behind the crank center, or bottom bracket. There's a frame tube (the seat tube) running from the cranks to the saddle, and it's at an angle. That angle partly determines the fore-aft position of the saddle, relative to the cranks and pedals. The fore-aft position in turn determines how your body is balanced on the bicycle. Your balance determines how comfortable you are, and how efficiently you can pedal the bike.

Stand up straight in front of a mirror and turn to the side. Look at yourself in the mirror. When standing straight, your head, hands, seat and feet are all fairly close to being in line with each other. Now bend over at the waist. Notice that not only has your head moved to a position ahead of your feet, but your rear end has also moved behind your feet. If this were not the case, you would fall forward. Your seat moves back when you bend at the waist to keep you in balance. Your torso needs to be leaning forward for two reasons: power output and aerodynamics. With an upright torso, you can't use the gluteus muscles to good effect. In addition, you can't pull up on the handlebar effectively from an upright position.

An upright torso is also very poor aerodynamically. When cycling on level ground, the majority of your effort goes against wind resistance. Obviously, the most aerodynamically efficient position may not be the most pleasant position to be in for long rides. So there's a tradeoff. As you move to a more horizontal position, the saddle needs to be positioned further to the rear to maintain your body's balance, just as your rear end moves to the rear as you bend over while standing. Racers are more inclined to use a horizontal torso position than tourers, and racers are more concerned with having the handlebars further forward to make climbing and sprinting out of the saddle more effective. As you move the saddle forward from that balanced position, you'll have more and more weight supported by your arms, but you'll be able to position the handlebars further forward for more power. The track sprinter has the frame built with a rather steep seat tube angle, which positions the saddle further forward than where the tourer would want it.

If you can't move your saddle forward enough or backward enough for the fit you want, don't despair. Different saddles position the rails further ahead than others, giving more or less saddle offset. Seat posts are available with the clamps in different positions relative to the centerline of the post as well.

You may have a bicycle for short fast rides, and another for long tours. Just as the two bikes will have different components suited to their respective functions, so the fit will be different. The rider hasn't changed. You are still you. But your purpose has changed. The light, fast bike for short rides will likely have a more forward and lower handlebar position than the tourer. And so the saddle may well be further forward too. As you move the saddle forward or backward, you are also changing the effective saddle height, relative to the cranks, since the saddle rails are usually not perpendicular to the seat tube. So be prepared to change the seat post extension as you adjust the fore-aft saddle position; lowering the saddle as you move it back to maintain the same leg extension, and raising it as you move the saddle forward.

Handlebar width and drop for Mæs bend bars

A few brands of drop style bars come with a choice of how much lower the drop section of the bar is from the top. Unless you are a track sprinter or a criterium racer, you don't need very deep drop bars. Most bars come in a selection of widths. Most people seem happiest with their hands positioned on the bar at about the same distance apart as the width of their shoulders, so that your arms are roughly parallel when reaching to the bar. When determining stem dimensions, try the different bar widths available, starting with one that's the same as your shoulders' width, and see which works best for you.

Frame sizing

Stems and seat posts come in lots of different configurations. That means you can choose from several different frame sizes and still get the same good fit. All other things being equal, a longer top tube will give you a bike with a longer wheelbase, less twitchy handling and better shock absorption, calling for a shorter reach stem. Since the down tube (which connects the bottom bracket with the head tube) will be longer, it can twist a bit more, making the frame somewhat less stiff while accelerating: a definite performance penalty.
A longer seat tube will allow for a higher handlebar position with the same stem, giving you more room for pumps and water bottles. It can also prevent you from getting as low a handlebar position as you may want. Most importantly though, the longer seat tube raises the top tube and decreases stand-over clearance, something you should give careful consideration to. Most of us want to be somewhere between the fit of the track racer's bike and the long distance tourer's bike. But, of course, each of us has to find our ideal point for ourselves. Remember, there is only one expert when it comes to fitting your bike.
Only you know how you feel on your bike. Only you know what compromises you are willing to make while riding.

Photo by Carson Ting
www.chairmanting.com

The Prescience of the Future
An interpretation of the bike frame
from old masters to the new wave of builders

Ian Sutton by Justin Keena

Cinelli **De Rosa** *Icarus*

The first model of "Supercorsa Lupi"

Cino Super Corsa Pista

Cinelli
The evolution of a myth

Cino Cinelli was a man in love with bikes. In the first years of his career, he took to racing, winning competitions such as the Milano-San Remo and the Giro di Lombardia.

His passion for cycling was second only to his passion for innovation, so he relocated to Milan—center of the Italian cycling industry—and founded his very own brand. At first, depending on bigger companies to manage his sales, he produced superb and innovative parts such as the modern handlebar, the plastic frame saddle, the first toe clips, and the first quick release pedals. But his frames were also very refined and precise, and became the official bikes for the 1968 Tokyo Olympics.

It's no wonder that Cinelli teamed up with Columbus, makers of the finest steel tubing for the cycling industry. Together, the two companies have been innovating bike design constantly for more than 50 years, from their LASER prototypes down to their base models.

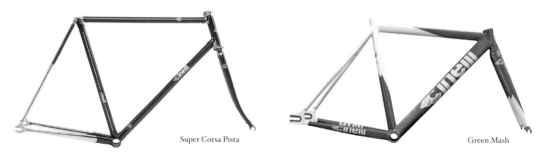

Super Corsa Pista   Green Mash

Cinelli Overall

The harmonious fusion of form and function has won this brand many design prizes, including the prestigious Compasso d'Oro, which is awarded each year to the most interesting industrial design project in Italy.

Cinelli's philosophy is to conceive the bike as a total project. Cycling and art are inextricably linked today, but Cinelli was a pioneer of this coupling. Back in 1979 the company's identity was re-interpreted by renowned Italian designer Italo Lupi, who created the famous "C" logo.

Cinelli is also well known for involving famous artists in the design process: Keith Haring, Barry McGee and Mike Giant, to name just a few. Cinelli's philosophy of combining art and sport, and its continuous passion for innovation, make it one of the most respected bike companies in the world.

The "C" logo designed in 1979 by the italian designer Italo Lupi

"Barry" model

"Laser Rivoluzione"

Laser

The Laser project is Cinelli's testing ground for new technologies in bicycle racing, and a continuation of the innovative Cinelli tradition. Over the years, this ongoing project has been the launch pad for many pioneering technical solutions, which have since become common property. 1979 saw the birth of the first T.I.G. welded. racing chassis, followed by the first box structure in paper thin chromium-molybdenum steel (1981), the first frame with bottom bracket axle (1982), the first monocoque carbon structure–and many more.

Laser "Evoluzione" and its seagull wing handlebar

"One has to know how to make bicycles before selling them"

Ugo De Rosa

De Rosa
An artisan disguised as a bike company

Many consider De Rosa to be one of the most prominent master frame builders in Italy and the world. Ugo De Rosa, the charismatic figure behind the brand name, is closely linked to the development of the Italian racing bicycle. Skillful and imaginative, his name is on the short-list of preeminent frame artists that were instrumental in reinforcing the quality associated with the "made in Italy" stamp in the 1960's.

Ugo De Rosa advocated a strict pragmatism in his pursuit of excellence. As he put it, "one has to know how to make bicycles before selling them", and this simple rule was instrumental in transforming his business from a small workshop to one of the finest companies in the cycling world.

Ugo De Rosa and sons
(to say nothing of the dog!)

Ugo De Rosa with
Eddie Merckx

Fast forward fifty years: the company is still family owned and De Rosa's production facilities—much like other Italian manufacturers—can be seen more as a guild of artisans than a factory. Every frame model is planned thoroughly, right down to the smallest detail. Everything is analyzed in lab tests, some of which are performed right in the factory, and others at university laboratories.

Static and dynamic tests are complemented by countless road assessments, carried out by both experienced professional racers and amateurs, all of whom are people with "explosive" legs, testers who are able to put a racing bike through its paces like few others can. Production starts only when the results exceed the parameters of resistance, safety and duration. Nothing in a De Rosa bike is mass produced, ensuring top quality for the brand throughout the world.

Their vintage frames are very hard to find: understandably, not many people want to sell them! However, if you're lucky enough to find one for sale, expect a four-figure price tag. In the last few years, in keeping with other major manufacturers, De Rosa has started to produce a fixed-gear/single speed version of its road frame.

Icarus
Passionate framemaking
words by *Ian Sutton*, photos by *Milica Wren* and *Justin Keena*

Ian Sutton began building frames early on in life, and his passion led him to attend the Yamaguchi Frame Building School in Rifle, Colorado. The training was 100% one-on-one with one of the greats in frame building. Koichi Yamaguchi taught the basics from start to finish, along with the more nuanced aspects of bike design. Ian went on to visit builders he admired and was offered a job working for the esteemed Seven Cycles in Watertown, MA. Ian left everything else behind and jumped headfirst into the frame building world, initially working as a finisher and later as machinist. When he felt he had enough experience under his belt, Ian started building his own concept frames and christened the project Icarus.

Icarus frames is now Ian's life–each frame is an opportunity to expand the look and design of Icarus. People aren't 'stock' so neither are his bikes–each one is crafted for the particular client, in terms of fit, ride characteristics and aesthetics.

The project

After measuring and interviewing the customer and finding more information about their current bike(s), I design and draft a full-scale frame drawing. This is used mostly during machining to get very accurate angles and lengths for tube coping. It also allows me to make more complicated design choices than most of the bike frame design computer programs out there.

Machining

I have no milling machines or lathes in my shop. Tubes are cut to length with a hacksaw then I use a bench grinder to start the cope. The bench grinder is a nice way to extend the life of my files but it's just the start to a good cope. I use hand files with a level and a machinist's protractor to achieve copes that are a perfect fit. They need to be at the correct angle, length and orientation to create a bike that matches the design, is in good alignment, and is very strong.

Tacking

Once all of the tubes are coped and cleaned thoroughly, I set them up in a frame jig to hold them in place for tacking. I use a specific sequence to ensure the frame will stay in alignment during brazing later. A viscous white goo or "flux" is applied to all the joints. It is used to keep the joint clean and allow the brazing material to flow nicely through the joint, it also acts as a temperature indicator so you know when the metal is at an optimal temperature.

Fillet Brazing

After tacking, I make notations about the frame alignment so that I can braze in a pattern that keeps everything straight. Fillet brazing requires more time than both TIG welding and lugged construction but the freedom of design and stunning finish more than makes up for the extra work. I do an internal and external fillet for supreme strength. Sometimes described as slow motion welding, it involves using a large amount of molten brass and using gravity to shape the fillet. Heat control is exceptionally important, too cold and you risk leaving voids and creating a segmented fillet, too hot and the fillets will just collapse and you could also damage and distort the steel itself.

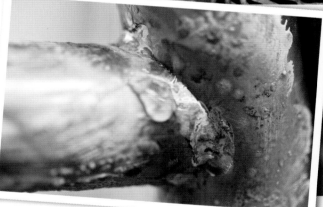

Finishing

Once the frame is fully brazed, I soak it in hot water to get rid of the flux, both inside and outside of the tubes. If left inside, the flux can corrode the tubing. I use hand files and sand paper to finish the frame. It takes many hours to get each fillet looking super smooth, using increasingly fine strips of sand paper. Some builders don't like finishing but it really rounds out the package of the custom frame that looks, fits and performs at a higher level.

Vanhulsteijn bicycles
Unusual geometries
www.vanhulsteijn.com

Designed and built by
Herman van Hulsteijn,
this bike has a TIG welded stainless
steel frame, 3 cm (1 in) forks, Hplusson
polished rims, Sturmey Archer 3-speed
fixed hub, Continental "grand prix"
tires, BLB track 48T crankset, and
Vanhulsteijn handlebars and frontbrake.

Pollo Design
Wooden detail
www.pollodesign.it

Coaster-pedal singlespeed. Entirely hand-built, oak wood veneered frame, ash wood wheels, calfskin saddle.

"When the only tool you have is a hammer, every problem begins to resemble a nail."

Abraham Maslow

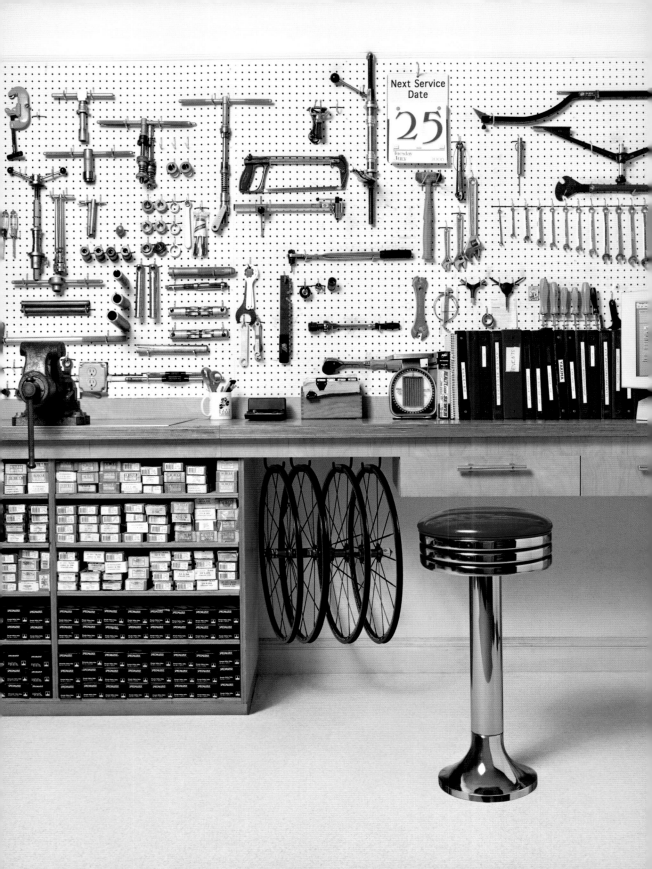

Next Service
Date
25
Tuesday
JULY 2009

Tools

A road-bike to single speed/fixed gear conversion can be done relatively cheaply, and most of the tools you'll need are standard equipment in any household. There are, however, some bike-specific tools that are essential to getting the job done easily and safely.

If you surf the web, you'll find many video "tutorials" on how to do this or that task without the specific tool. Most of the time, the methods decribed are pure monkey business, and will put your bike part (and your hands) at risk. If you find yourself tempted to use a combination of hammer and screwdrivers to remove or install something, with the goal of saving some money, think again. You'll probably mess up the piece, strip the threading, and need to buy a replacement piece, wasting more money than you would've spent on the tool in the first place.

None of the specific tools listed here are very expensive, and most communal workshops or bike shops which will rent them out for a fraction of the retail price. But you must bear in mind that working on bikes is highly addictive; odds are that once you're done with your first conversion you'll feel the urge to do many more!

Bikeshop by Frank Schott
www.frankschott.com

Bikeshop by Olesya Shchukina
appleandcloud@gmail.com

Dad, Rhys Logan

Cable cutter

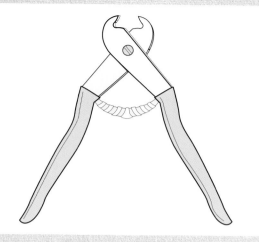

A cable cutter will see a lot of use during a bike conversion, considering the amount of cables you'll have to get rid of. But, more importantly, a cable cutter is needed to cut brake housing cables precisely.

OPTIONAL

Chain tool

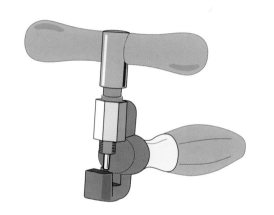

Bicycle chains are held together by pins, and there is no way of taking them apart easily, except with a chain tool.
They are very inexpensive (but watch out for really cheap ones that give you too little leverage).

REQUIRED

Chainring nut wrench

This tool can occasionally be substituted with a big flathead screwdriver, but in most situations it is essential for chainring bolt installation and removal. It holds the slotted nut securely in place to prevent spinning when tightening or loosening the bolt.

REQUIRED

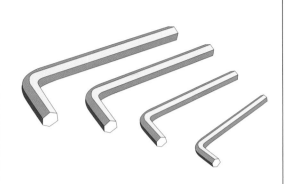

Hex wrenches

Most of the components on bikes are fastened using 4mm, 5mm or 6mm allen bolts. Specific three-way hex wrenches are available in bike shops, but it's best to keep a set of long allen keys on hand, as you will occasionally need some extra sizes like an 8mm for crank bolts, and a ball-end that makes it easy to spin long bolts quickly.

REQUIRED

Crescent wrench

Most bike parts are not screwed on very tight. A crescent wrench is a good option for many parts, although it should be used with caution.

REQUIRED

Hammer

Some components will need to be taper fit or pressure fit. A hammer is the good tool for this. It's best to get a two-sided head, with both a steel and rubber striking surface.

REQUIRED

Bottom Bracket lockring wrench
(general purpose)

Older bicycles will most likely have a standard lockring keeping the adjustable cup in place. The adjustable caps come in many shapes and aren't threaded on very tightly, so they're usually pretty easy to remove.

OPTIONAL

Bottom Bracket lockring wrench
(bike specific)

Through the years, different manufacturers have introduced many different types of bottom bracket lockrings. Make sure to have the appropriate type for your bike.

REQUIRED

Bottom bracket fixed cup wrench

The fixed cup is screwed in very tight, even more so in French and Italian frames. It's almost impossible to remove a fixed cup without the proper tool.

REQUIRED

Tools, Gaëtan Rossier
www.gaetanrossier.ch

Cone & pedal wrenches

Cone wrenches are thin tools (2 mm), purpose-built to service and adjust the cones and adjustment nuts found on axles. Cone wrenches usually come in 13x14 millimeter, 15 x16 millimeter, and 17x18 millimeter sizes. You should have at least one but preferably two of each size needed for your hubs.

Usually standard open-end or adjustable wrenches are OK for cone locknuts, but cones can only be properly adjusted with thin cone wrenches.

Pedal wrenches are a little more heavy duty, and typically have longer handles because of the torque required for proper installation and removal..

REQUIRED

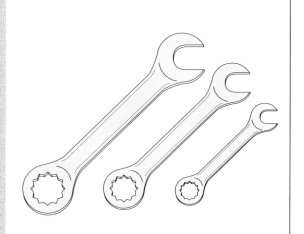

Open & closed-end wrenches

Most components are between 8mm and 17mm in size, so a good set of open-end wrenches is a must. It's also a good idea to have a couple of adjustable wrenches on hand for odd jobs, but use the proper size whenever possible, as adjustable wrenches often slip and can damage your bolts.

REQUIRED

IRO Mark V, Adam Thrower

Pliers

As for the hammer and the crescent wrench, a good set of pliers is always handy, as it will help you out in situations where you're likely to get stuck.

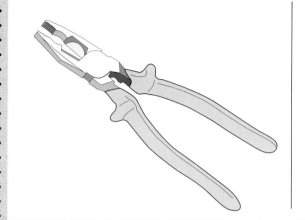

REQUIRED

Fourth hand

A 4th hand is very useful in brake installation. It grasps the inner cable and pulls it tight, maintaining its tension while the anchor-bolt is tightened.

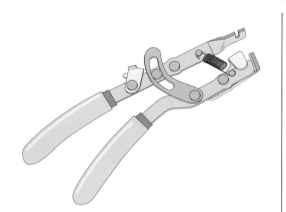

OPTIONAL

Spoke wrench

To re-dish the wheel and tighten the spokes, you will need a spoke wrench. They are usually color coded for size, but be sure to bring the bike or wheel to the shop to buy the correct size.

REQUIRED

Credits:

1. MyORB issue 3
This photography publication
revolves around classic
Japanese Keirin racing.
www.myorangebox.com
3. Annamarie Cabarloc
www.iminusd.com
2-4-5-6. *Fixed Gear in Bologna*,
photos by Luca Gambi

photo by Jake Marx

Crank puller

This tool screws into the dustcap threads, and the lever puts pressure on the end of the spindle, removing the cranks. Inexpensive versions don't come with the handle and should be used in conjunction with a crescent wrench. There are different sizes, so make sure to get the correct one.

OPTIONAL

Lubricants

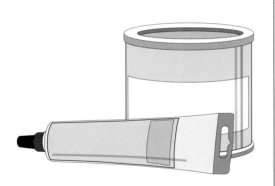

Three basic types of lubrication are needed: chain oil, light oil and, most importantly, waterproof grease.

Almost any grease will do, since the loads and temperatures are generally low.

REQUIRED

Screwdrivers

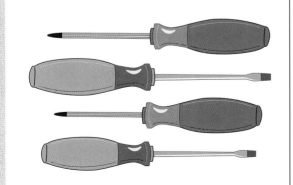

Both flathead and Phillips (+) screwdrivers are used regularly in a single speed/fixed-gear conversion.

REQUIRED

Skull Bike Club Spokecard by Mark Skulls
www.markskulls.com

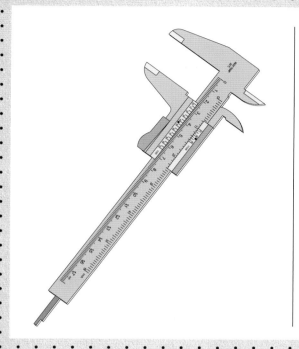

Meter & Caliper

Measuring tools are needed for a number of operations. While a standard meter is sufficient for most of these, when precision is essential a caliper will be needed.

REQUIRED

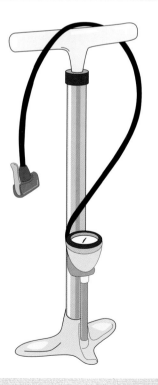

Pump

A pump is an essential piece of equipment for any bicyclist.

Investing in a good pump will save you time. The best ones are upright floor pumps with both Presta/French and Schrader/American valves. A pressure gauge is also a very helpful feature.

REQUIRED

Photo by Brad Serls

Illustration by Matt Taylor
www.matttaylor.co.uk

Disassembly

In this chapter you'll learn how to take apart your newly acquired bicycle. Disassembly is relatively easy unless you encounter stubborn parts, but there is usually a way to remove them. As always, the best strategy is to keep your tools handy at all times, and to have a big enough space to contain everything, otherwise you run the risk of losing important parts as you reassemble your bike.

Most operations are pretty straightforward, whether it's a question of unscrewing, unthreading or pulling out. A good bike mechanic will tell you that it's possible to disassemble a bike in less than an hour, but until you feel confident, the best thing is to take it easy, and concentrate on understanding how it all fits together.

Complete disassembly is a fundamental part of the conversion of a bike, because it allows you to inspect all the parts and clean them thoroughly. It also gives you confidence in the bike itself. Just like that frog you dissected in junior high, removing nuts, bolts and gears will reveal a new world, shedding light on the form and function of the bicycle as a simple machine.

Photos by Annemarie Cabarloc
www.iminusd.com

Bike Parts, by Karl Addison
www.idrawalot.com

Removing the seat

The first step in bike disassembly is usually to take the seat off.
A metric allen wrench and/or a regular hexwrench will be needed to unscrew the nut and bolt. Usually only one side is meant to turn, while the other side has a tab fixed on the frame, so be careful to unscrew the right side.

The seat post is normally fitted very tightly into the seat tube, and it can take serious effort to unscrew it. A way to apply more force is to pin your knee on the rear wheel and twist the seat upwards.

The seat post might have scratches on it. In this case, the inside of the seat tube should be filed and smoothed.

Cutting the cables

Cables used on older bicycles are conventional spiral housing cables. The internal wire is made of twisted strands of steel. The outer housing is wound in a spiral and the wire runs through the housing.

It's a good idea to start clipping the cables, using a cable cutter or any other suitable tool. Most wire isn't reusable anyways and it's not expensive to buy it new.

Photo by Damiano Merlo

The cables have to be clipped just above the brake parts right before they terminate.

Underneath the front derailleur there is an open section of cable that can be clipped.

Removing handlebars & stem

Next step in disassembly are the handlebar stem and the handlebars. The stem is the part that holds the handlebars on the steerer tube of the fork.

The stems of most bicycles with threaded headsets fit inside the steerer tube of the fork, and are attached to the steerer by means of an expander/wedge. The wedge is secured by an allen-head bolt (hex wrench).

Photo by Christian Webber
www.chriswebber.ca

Photo by Alex Pink
www.snapshotlondon.co.uk

Stuck or stubborn stems

The wedge expander locks the stem at the right height, but it may be stuck in there if the bike hasn't been serviced in a while. A trick to get around this is to tap the hex-socket bolt lightly with a hammer (after unscrewing the bolt) to break it free.

If the stem is particularly stubborn, it's a good idea to lubricate the headset.

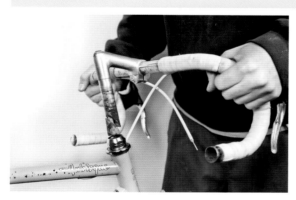

The handlebar should be removed by holding the front wheel between your legs and twisting upwards in both directions.

Once the handlebar has been removed, you might find that more brake cables have to be clipped.

Handlebars

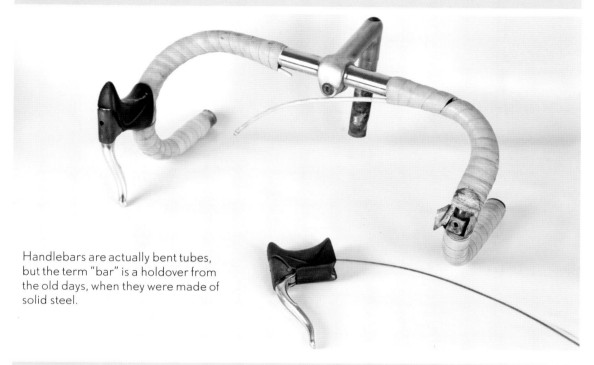

Handlebars are actually bent tubes, but the term "bar" is a holdover from the old days, when they were made of solid steel.

Brake levers

The brake levers must be removed. They are held in place by a clamp tightened by a screw inside the lever housing. To gain access to that screw you have to squeeze the brake lever.

Most handlebars will be outfitted with dust-caps that keep dirt out and the bar-ends safe and smooth.

Photo by Kai Streets
www.kaistreets.com

above: Tina Tru aka Tinaballs @ SJF/iMiNUSD alley cat, "Relationship" series.
below: on the bike: John Nguyen (sponsored IMD rider), J.P. Flores and Tricia Vasquez.
Photos by Annemarie Cabarloc - *www.iminusd.com*

Handlebar dustcaps have to be pulled out in order to remove the handlebar tape.

Handlebar tape is usually made of cloth or plastic. On an old bike, it is usually in bad shape, so no use recycling it unless it's made of leather.

Once the handlebar tape is off, you can loosen the hex-socket stem screw further, and slide the stem free from the handlebars.

Carefully work the stem off the handlebars. You may have to pry the stem open slightly with a screwdriver to avoid gouging the handlebar tubing.

Stem

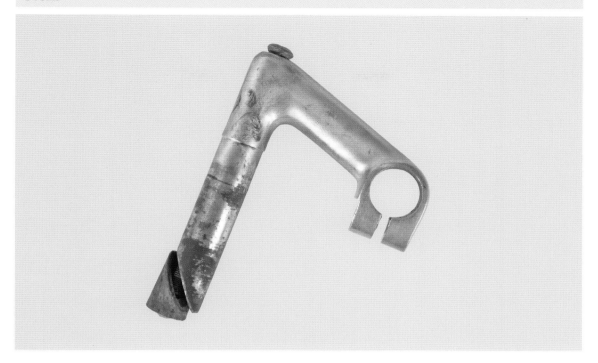

The stem is a very important part of the bike, as it supports a big fraction of the weight of the rider through his/her arms and hands. If you notice a lot of wear and/or the stem is of low quality, it might be a good idea to shop for a new one.

Stems for bikes with threaded headsets are usually made to fit inside the fork steerer. The stem diameter matches exactly the inside of the steerer, so it comes to about 3mm less than the nominal headset size.

Threadless stems

Another common stem type is the threadless stem. These are more modern and usually mounted on higher end bikes.

These are made of three parts including the headset, and are easily removed by unscrewing the pinch bolts and the top cap bolt.

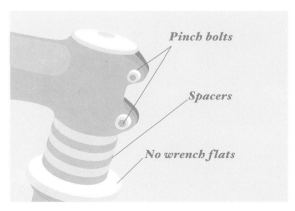

Pinch bolts

Spacers

No wrench flats

CATCH UP

Caliper brakes

Most road bikes use mount caliper brakes, with shoes mounted inward towards the rim. A side-pulled caliper brake (*a*) uses a single arm to move both brakes, while a center-pull brake is a caliper brake in which the main cable runs down the center line of the bicycle, using a yoke to connect to a transverse cable.

This type of brake was fashionable from the late 1960's to the early 1980's. Center-pull brakes (*b*) are a good choice for bicycles which have a long reach from the mounting point to the rim. And some might be worth keeping, especially if you want to give your bike a vintage look.

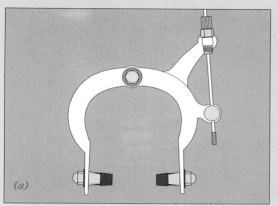

(*a*)

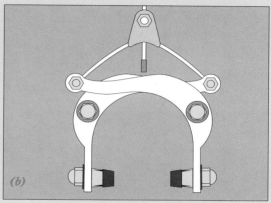

(*b*)

Removing the front brake

All brakes are held in place by a single nut and bolt.

Loosen the bolt and the brakes should be easy to remove.

The big race by Matthew Hodson
www.matthewthehorse.co.uk/

Removing the rear brake

The rear brake is easily removed once the fixing post is unscrewed.

Brakes are easily re-used, so don't throw them away. Get rid of the sharp inner cable and store them away for later use.

Removing other components

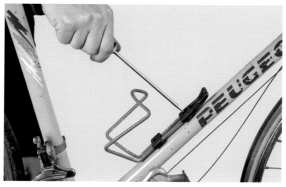

All superfluous accessories, such as the bottle holder, should be removed.

Next in the disassembly line are the shifters. If the cable clipping was done correctly, it is just a matter of loosening a bolt.

Photos by Dave Alexander

Shifters

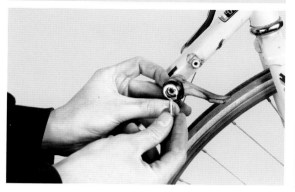

On this particular model, the shifters bolt onto posts welded on the downtube. Some models are held together by means of a metal band around tubing.

Derailleur

A derailleur is a mechanism for shifting the chain from one cog to another on multi-speed bicycles, usually attached directly onto the right dropout.

The derailleur will most probably be held in place by one hex nut or a hex-socket bolt. Loosen this to remove the derailleur.

This particular frame had a dropout with an integrated rear-derailleur hanger. Sometimes hangers sit underneath the axle bolts, and they must be removed along with the derailleur (see Dropouts).

 Polo Night by Jesse Brew
http://aroundaround.com

Removing the chain

To remove the chain, position it across the slotted jaws of the chain tool, so that one of the chain pins aligns with the slot. Then screw the pin extractor until the mandrel comes into contact with the chain pin. Make sure everything is aligned perfectly, and then start turning the handle whilst pushing out the pin. Always stop when the pin is hanging out of the side plate opposite to it.

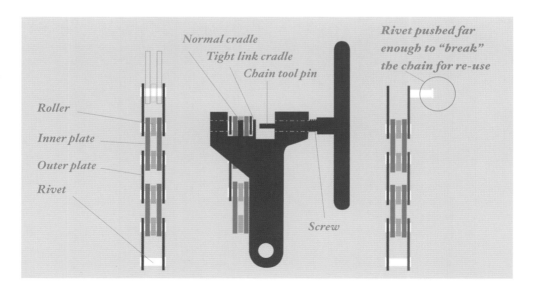

Normal cradle
Tight link cradle
Chain tool pin
Rivet pushed far enough to "break" the chain for re-use
Roller
Inner plate
Outer plate
Rivet
Screw

Using the chaintool

Next up is the chain. To remove the chain there is a special tool called a chain-remover. Any other ways to remove a chain are dangerous and ineffective, so it's worth buying the correct tool. It should not be very expensive.

Don't push the pin all the way out. If you do, it's very tricky to get it back in. Once you've broken one chain link it's easy to pull it out.

A 3/32" chain is used on almost all road bikes, but most single gear bikes use 1/18".

Removing the front derailleur

Removing the pedal

The front derailleur is made of two metal plates that shift sideways to push the chain from one chainring to another. They are usually held in place by a mounting clamp locked by a nut and bolt.

Most of the time pedals can be removed by means of a regular wrench. However, some pedals may require a thinner, longer wrench to unscrew them (not surprisingly called a pedal-wrench).

Keep in mind that the drive-side (right side) pedal unscrews in the regular direction (CCL) while the left pedal is threaded backwards (CL).

Credits:

1. *Stop Honking* t-shirt by MyORB
www.myorangebox.com
2-10. 林 辰崎 aka Zzhi
3. Will Manville
www.willmanville.com/
4. Gaëtan Rossier
www.gaetanrossier.ch
5. Wilis Johnson
6. *Color Theory*,
by Karl Addison
www.idrawalot.com
7. Noor Azlan Mohamed
8. Dave Alexander
9. Taylor Hurley
of Mobius Cycle
11. Edward Pepper

Pedals

To remove "frozen" pedals from an aluminum crank, remove the crank and pedal from the BB spindle and try heating the pedal end of the crank over a gas flame. Using a pedal wrench, the pedal usually unscrews relatively easily without damage. If a lubricated pedal with clean threads does not screw in easily, a thread tap should be run through the crank to prevent galling on insertion. You're better off doing it on the bicycle, where the crank is held firmly by the BB and prevented from rotation by the chain. To keep chain tension to a minimum (so the rear wheel does not spin), keep the pedal wrench as parallel to the crank as possible, rather than as an extension of the crank.

Removing the crank

After removing the dustcaps, the cranks should reveal either nuts or bolts threaded onto the spindle stud. A thin socket wrench or a crank removal tool should be used to unscrew the nuts.

The crank removal tool fits snugly into the crank socket, and enables you to use a wrench to unscrew the crank bolts or nuts.

The big race by Matthew Hodson
www.matthewthehorse.co.uk

Cranks

On many older and/or low-end bicycles, the cranks are attached to the bottom bracket axle by means of cylindrical wedges called cotters. These are usually pressed in, and have a nut to secure them.

If the bike is old and dirty and hasn't been serviced in a long time, the cotters will usually be very difficult to remove.

There are many ways to remove stubborn cotters. The first option is to use a cotter pin press, which is essentially a c-shaped press that should eject the cotter from the socket easily. However, this doesn't always work, so the next option is usually to use a hammer. When attempting this, place a support stretching from the floor to the crank. The pipe will transmit the impact of the hammer to the ground, preventing damage to the bearing cups and axle cones.

A crank removal tool works by threading into the dustcap threads. Turning the lever exerts force on the end of the spindle, thereby forcing the cranks off the bottom bracket spindle..

A crank removal tool is undoubtedly the most effective way to remove cranks, but cheaper options do exist: Sometimes it is possible to use a soft-top hammer, as shown, to push the cranks off, but it could damage the spindle as well as the cranks themselves, so take care with this.

Photo by Dave Alexander

Damaged threads

If the crank threads are damaged, not all hope is lost. Begin by inspecting the threads.

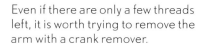

Even if there are only a few threads left, it is worth trying to remove the arm with a crank remover.

If the threads are completely stripped, the arm is basically ruined.

If the cranks are stubborn, a simple repair option involves trying to clean the threads. There are tools to do this; they will align damaged and cross-threaded threads, but not cut out new ones.

If the threads are completely stripped, the arm is basically ruined.

At this point you can try various things to remove them:
Pedaling the bike after removing the nuts is a good way to remove the cranks, but it should be done uphill and with caution.

If nothing else works, destructive removal will be your only option.

You can use a hacksaw to cut into the arm at the spindle joint. A cold chisel can then be used to split the arm.

The powertrain is usually the grimiest part of the bike as well as the easiest to see, so it's a good idea to take everything apart to clean before reassembly.

Bottom bracket removal

The bottom bracket is usually removed starting from the left, or non-drive, side. An adjustable cup has to be adjusted to just the right tension, and is held in place by means of a lockring.

Lockring

Different bottom brackets will have different configurations, but for older bikes this is the most common set-up. A specific lockring tool is used to unscrew it, although it's also possible to get it off in other, less orthodox ways.

Adjustable cup

The adjustable cup is threaded to the right inside the bottom bracket shell, so you will have to turn conventionally (CCL) to unscrew it. Some bottom brackets can be unscrewed with a normal wrench, whilst others will have different configurations, but they won't be more than finger tight, so it's easy to remove them

Photo by Dave Alexander

Bearings

The cup should be unscrewed with the greatest caution, because it's important not to lose the bearings that run in the cup.

Traditional cup-and-cone bearings will be found on older bikes. Most bikes have 9 or 11 bearings on both sides of the bottom bracket.

STAY AHEAD

Spindle

The most logical way to go is to replace the most worn out ones, as they are very inexpensive. Ball bearings should not be mixed, though, as they might differ from batch to batch. These microscopic differences, as well as pits and scratches in the bottom brackets, are surprisingly significant when it comes to proper drive-train functioning.

Fixed cup

The right, or drive side cup is the "fixed cup", and it usually has a collar or flange that reaches the edge of the bottom bracket shell when in position. This cup should be in very tight, so a specific tool is required. In English/ISO bikes, the fixed cup is threaded backwards (left) to prevent unscrewing as a result of pedaling. Italian and older French bikes are threaded normally.

Bottom bracket

Once everything has been taken apart, you should have all the parts laid out and ready to be cleaned.

Components of a typical headset

The structure that connects the fork to the frame is called a headset.

There are both threadless and threaded headsets, and the latter are the ones which are found on older bikes.

A standard threaded headset consists of four races plus associated parts:

a) The adjustable top race
b) The upper head race, pressed into the top of the head tube
c) The lower head race, pressed into the bottom of the head tube
d) The crown race

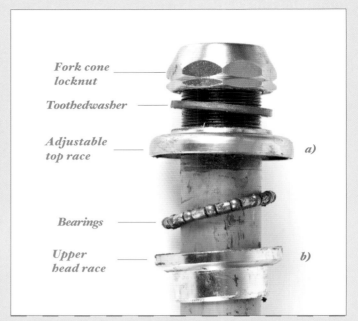

Fork cone locknut
Toothedwasher
Adjustable top race — *a)*
Bearings
Upper head race — *b)*

Frame head tube

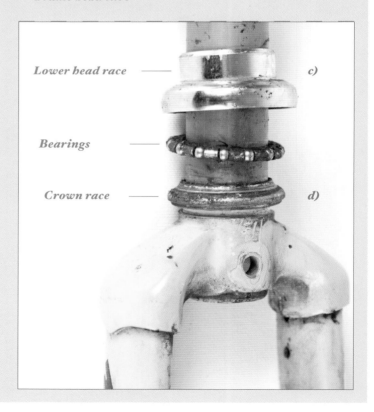

Lower head race — *c)*
Bearings
Crown race — *d)*

Headset disassembly

Headset disassembly is a pretty straightforward procedure. The fork cone locknut usually has a standard hex profile.

Occasionally, it will have a pin or other type of locknut, but it shouldn't be tightly threaded.

The rest of the headset elements should be screwed in finger-tight, so they shouldn't present a problem for removal.

The upper and lower head races fit in the steer tube very tightly, and should be pressed in. A simple tap with a screwdriver will do the trick.

There are specific tools to do this, but there's no danger of ruining the steel components of old bikes as long as you're careful not to scratch the actual bearing surfaces.

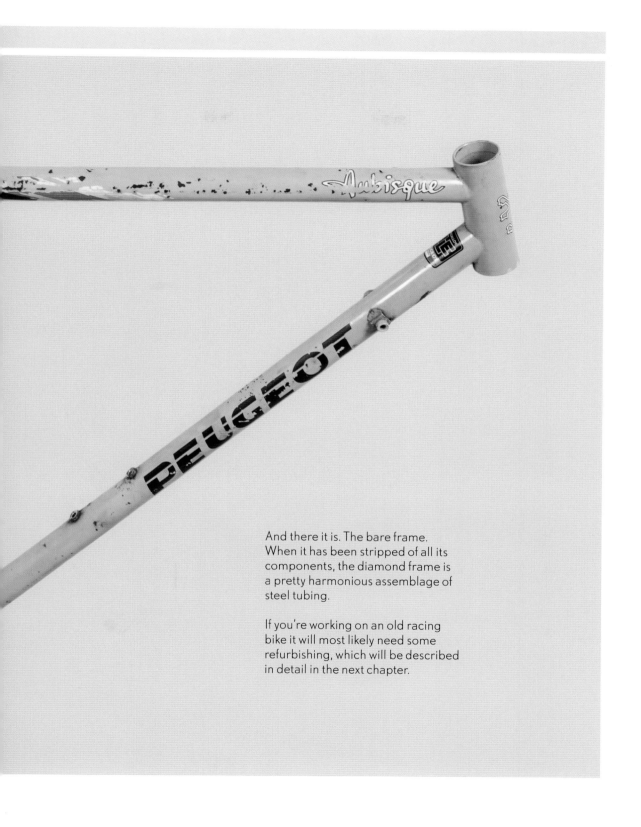

And there it is. The bare frame. When it has been stripped of all its components, the diamond frame is a pretty harmonious assemblage of steel tubing.

If you're working on an old racing bike it will most likely need some refurbishing, which will be described in detail in the next chapter.

Photo by Luca Gambi
www.lucagambi.com

Matt W. Moore - MWM Graphics
http://mwmgraphics.com

THIS IS

BICY

THIS IS

Restoring

Restoration is an exceptionally challenging and time-consuming job, and it requires bucketloads of dedication and persistence. Depending on the initial state of the bike you choose to convert, you will go from needing just a few scrubs with mineral spirits to an entire make-over: refurbishing is a term that can assume a pretty wide range of meanings. Most retouching can be done at home with a good dose of savvy and lots of scrubbing. It's a lengthy process that can be repetitive at times, and it certainly demands lots of stamina. But the rewards far outweigh the occasional tedium of the process!

Although a complete and thorough cleaning of the frame and components is a must, repainting is a different issue. It's not too difficult to achieve a good result, but home paintjobs are always thinner and less durable. Professional paint shops have access to special paints and temperature-controlled ovens. Moreover, from an aesthetic point of view, conserving the original paintjob leaves the bike with a vintage feel, difficult to achieve with a new one!

Photo by Jake Marx

Abstract by Karl Addison
www.idrawalot.com

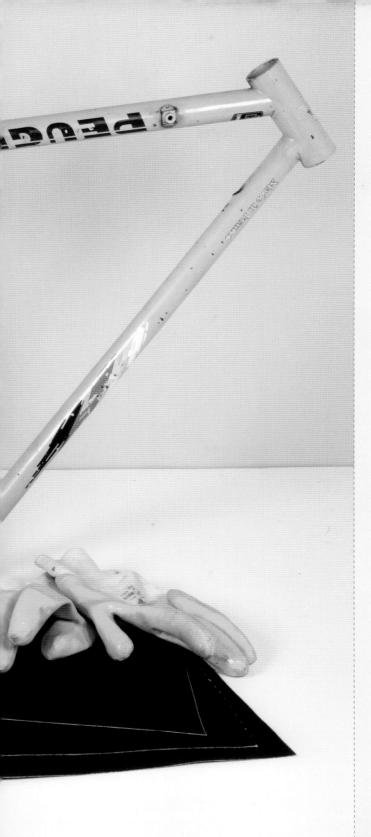

DIY Refurbishing
Essential tools

- **Sandpaper**
  Have different grades on hand

- **Paint stripper**

- **Protective wear**
  Some of the chemicals that are used at this stage of preparation are toxic and extremely irritating: goggles, gloves and clothing that protect the skin are essential

- **Putty knife / steel spatula**
  Very handy when removing the paint stripper

- **Brush**
  To apply the paint stripper

- **Steel polishing brush**

- **Metal polish**

- **Metal filler**

- **Lacquer**

- **Masking tape**

Polafixie, Gaëtan Rossier
www.gaetanrossier.ch

How to touch up rust and chipped paint

by Rasmus Folehave Hansen - *www.refurbs.blogspot.com*

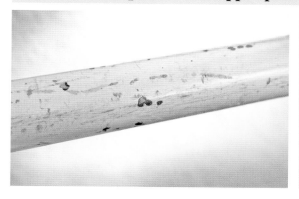 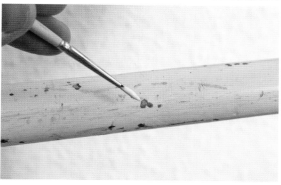

Using fine sandpaper, remove all signs of rust. Make sure that the edges of the hole are smooth and level with the surrounding paint. Clean thoroughly with ethanol or another solvent, then apply primer, paint and laquer.

Small paint chips can usually be disguised using a fine brush and a drop of paint of matching color.

How to treat chrome parts

by Rasmus Folehave Hansen - *www.refurbs.blogspot.com*

Surface rust can be removed from chrome parts quite easily. Take a piece of tinfoil and crumble it into a loose ball. Apply a small amount of fluid to make the rubbing process easier.

🐇 Ethanol, window cleaner or whatever you have handy works just fine.

Gently rub the affected areas with the tinfoil, and the rust will disappear. This leaves the chrome a bit dull, but if you want, it can be repolished to a beautiful shine.

🐇 If the rust has penetrated the chrome all the way to the steel, only a new chroming will restore the lustre.

Record by Andrey Maximovich

Applying the paint stripper

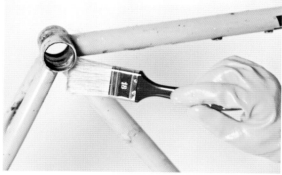

🖝 Paint stripper is a chemical product that "melts" paint so that it lifts off the surface to which it is applied.

It is generally very toxic and will irritate the skin, so apply it using a brush with gloves and a particulate (air-purifying) mask.

Apply a generous amount around joints.

The paint stripper will have to be left until the paint starts to detach itself from the frame.

Removing the existing paint

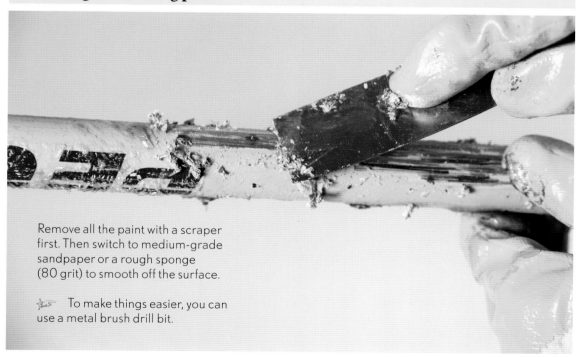

Remove all the paint with a scraper first. Then switch to medium-grade sandpaper or a rough sponge (80 grit) to smooth off the surface.

🖝 To make things easier, you can use a metal brush drill bit.

Photo by Azlan Mohamed

Paintless frame

When the paint is all stripped away, the frame is ready to be repainted.

Repairing dents

If you need to take a break of more than a few days, make sure to store the bike in a dry place: when it's stripped down like this, rust can form very easily.

If there are any dents or wear marks which you want to fill in, this is the time to do it. You can use knifing putty, bondo, or something similar to produce a smooth surface. Make sure that you sand it down well afterwards, and remove the dust.

Hang the bike to make sure no part of it escapes your attention.

🖙 If you don't have a stand, you can hang it from a branch, or from the ceiling. Be creative...

🖙 All painting should be done in a well ventilated and lit area.

Masking tape

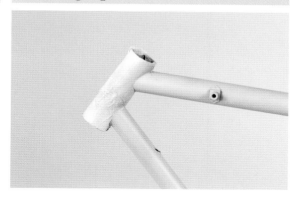

If there are any areas that don't need to be painted, make sure to cover them with masking tape.

🖙 The same technique can be used to paint different parts of the bike in different colors.

Credits:

1-2. Bryan Smith
3. Wilis Johnson
4. Simone Artale
5-8. Taylor Hurley for
Mobius Cycle
6. Edward Pepper
7. Levi Baer

Photo by Joseph R. Webb

Applying the primer

The primer protects the frame from rust and is the optimal surface for painting onto.

Primers vary in relation to the final color. Buy the primer according to your final color.

Spray about 20cm from the surface (or follow the instructions on the can). Start on hard to reach places like the head tube and bottom bracket.

Apply the primer 4 or 5 times in very thin coats, waiting 15-20 minutes between each one.
Allow the frame to dry for 24 hours.

🪶 Fresh primer is easily nicked, so, as much possible, don't move or touch the bike until it's totally dry.

Sanding the primer

Sand the primer using 220-grit paper/sponge. This is needed to achieve a gripping, porous surface to which the next layer of paint can adhere.

🪶 Be careful not to sand through the primer!

Main coat of paint

After cleaning the frame of dust, you're ready for the main coat of paint. Apply thin coats to achieve a uniform finish. Make sure to wait 15-20 minutes between coats.

Sanding the paint

After letting the paint dry for 24 hours, it's ready for another sanding.

☞ Use 1200-1500 grit paper or else you'll sand through the paintjob.

In order to avoid "loading" or "clogging" the sandpaper sheet should be lubricated with water and a bit of soap or degreaser.

This lubrication is especially important for sanding finish coats, since ordinary paper would clog quickly, rendering it useless.

The wet-sanding will allow the lacquer to stick better and give you a matte finish.

Decals and lacquer

Stickers or decals are optional, but the lacquer you put on afterward will protect the stickers.

☞ If you want to buy decals, have a look online, as there are many replicas of major bike manufacturers' labels.

Apply the clear lacquer in the same way as you painted the bike, but this time you may only need to put on 3 or 4 coats. It is important, especially at this stage, that you do not hold the spray can too far from the surface, as you could end up with a rough surface.

Wait about 5 minutes between lacquer coats, it could start to cure and form bubbles, resulting in bubbles in the next coat. Although it may look dry, it is better to leave the frame to rest for some days before reassembling it.

Decals

Decals fall into two major categories: the first are applied over the finished coat, the second, stuck onto the base coat and then protected with the clear coat.

They are further subdivided based on the method of application. There are four main types:

Varnish type

These decals are printed on duplex paper. One sheet is used as a guide to position the decal, and the other as a support. The sheets must be separated, before transferring, by rubbing a corner of the transfer.

Dry Fix

Peel off the thin backing paper. Apply the sticky side to the surface and rub downwards, applying extra pressure on the end from which the backing paper will be peeled. Leave for ten seconds, and peel off the backing paper gently. Rub down again for maximum adhesion. These decals have to be clearcoated.

Water Slide

Also known as waterdip transfers. To apply, soak them in water for not more than thirty seconds. When the decal comes off, slide it off into position. Press down well, wiping gently from the center outwards to squeeze out surplus water and air bubbles. The transfer won't set until dry, so you have some scope for correction after putting it into position. Leave at least 24 hours to dry and clearcoat.

Peel and Stick

Your common sticker. Remove backing paper, position transfer and rub down.

Customization

by Matt W. Moore - MWM Graphics - *http://mwmgraphics.com*

Process and materials

If you're repainting your bike, why not try your hand at a custom paint pattern? The possibilities are endless, and as long as you remember to apply darker colors first you can go wild with different combinations.

Masking the different parts is essential. Make sure to buy high quality masking tape and to wait for a sufficient amount of time between applying each successive color.

Spray paint is available in a wide variety of colors, you'll need at least two cans for the main coat, and another one for the smaller details.

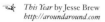
This Year by Jesse Brew
http://aroundaround.com

Polishing and Ordering

Mineral spirits will help you degrease all metal components.

🐁 Remember to keep everything in order! It's easy to lose track of small parts when the bike is disassembled.

Matt W. Moore - MWM Graphics

http://mwmgraphics.com
http://mwmgraphics.blogspot.com

Matt W. Moore is the founder of MWM Graphics, a design and illustration studio based in Portland, Maine. Matt works across disciplines, from colorful digital illustrations in his signature "Vectorfunk" style, to freeform watercolor paintings, to massive aerosol murals. MWM exhibits his artwork in galleries all around the world, and collaborates with clients in all disciplines. Matt is also co-founder and designer for Glyph Cue Clothing.

Chorus Gallery

Interview with Joshua Kampa - curator and proprietor of Arc-En-Ciel Bycicle Studio, Boston

Tell us about Chorus Gallery and its intent.

The gallery was started as a stand-alone but associated art space within OPEN Bicycle. Originally conceived as a separate business, it became rapidly apparent that the cross-cultural possibilities of the space were immense. Shows within the space bring art from many different subcultural areas to the community members attending the openings and exhibits as well as the day-to-day cycling community that passes through the shop. Intent and the organic reality of any project are different things–Chorus has evolved to become a different creature than originally designed, and now encompasses art shows, pop-up events, public works, and design-at-large.

Chorus works a lot with bike-related artists. Is this purely a coincidence, or are you trying to specialize in that field?

Chorus doesn't have an exclusive cycling-related mission, but the constant exchange between the cycling community and the greater art community upon the stage that Chorus represents means that there seems to be a consistent, if not always overt, cycling culture influence.

What trends do you see developing at the moment? Are more artists being influenced by bike culture?

Currently, there seems to be a good bit of bike-related momentum in the street art scene–renowned artists such as Futura, Stash, and Matthew Moore (who held a show at Chorus and painted a mural on the exterior of the building) are finding inspiration in the culture of urban cycling and have become influences for how the greater cycling community represents itself through art and image.

But I don't think it's a trend. Cyclists have always counted a number of aesthetes in their numbers, and artists and designers have been in turn influenced by the elements of personal freedom, velocity, and minimalism inherent in the world of cycling.

Do you think it can work both ways? Can art can contribute to the spreading of the bike as a way of life?

If we consider art as more than an aesthetic veneer for our contemporary lives and start to use it as a tool for urban development and morphological intentionality, I see a great potential for the "cycling movement" to become a larger cultural actor. As we begin to emerge from the legacy of Moses and Le Corbusier and rediscover a more Jacobsian "on-the-street" urban experience, cycling plays a natural role in metropolitan transportation infrastructure and hence the lived cultural experience of its inhabitants. The interplay between bicycles, the infrastructure that supports and encourage their use, and the changing overall urban environment and its pace and feel becomes a fecund space for artists, designers, urban planners, and community members to engage in an active reconfiguration of the utility and aesthetics of their cities.

Do you regard this current single-speed / fixed-gear hype as a positive thing? What do you see as its strong points and weaknesses?

I believe the overall impact of the excitement surrounding fixed-gear culture is extremely positive. The simplicity and sexiness of the bikes offers an easy entry-point into cycling for young riders. OPEN Bicycle seeks to foster an environment of inclusivity within a broader cycling community that welcomes all types of riders. Naturally, there are elements of territorialism and posturing present in the scene–however, I see these as representations of protectiveness and feel that they can be carefully subverted from within the community to become feelings of pride and empowerment for all involved.

Could you tell us about Spoke Count?

Spoke Count was an experiment at crowd-sourcing an art show. Rather than
a typical juried group show, the exhibit featured every piece of work that was
submitted. The call-for-work was simple: the piece had to fit in a 20 x 20cm
square space, be capable of being hung from a wall, and have some (if perhaps
only the vaguest) reference to cycling. Work was tiled in the gallery as it came in.
The community became the artist, the promoter, and the audience for the show,
and the end result was a pixelated introspection of the Boston cycling culture.
Spoke Count was by and large the most successful show to-date at Chorus.

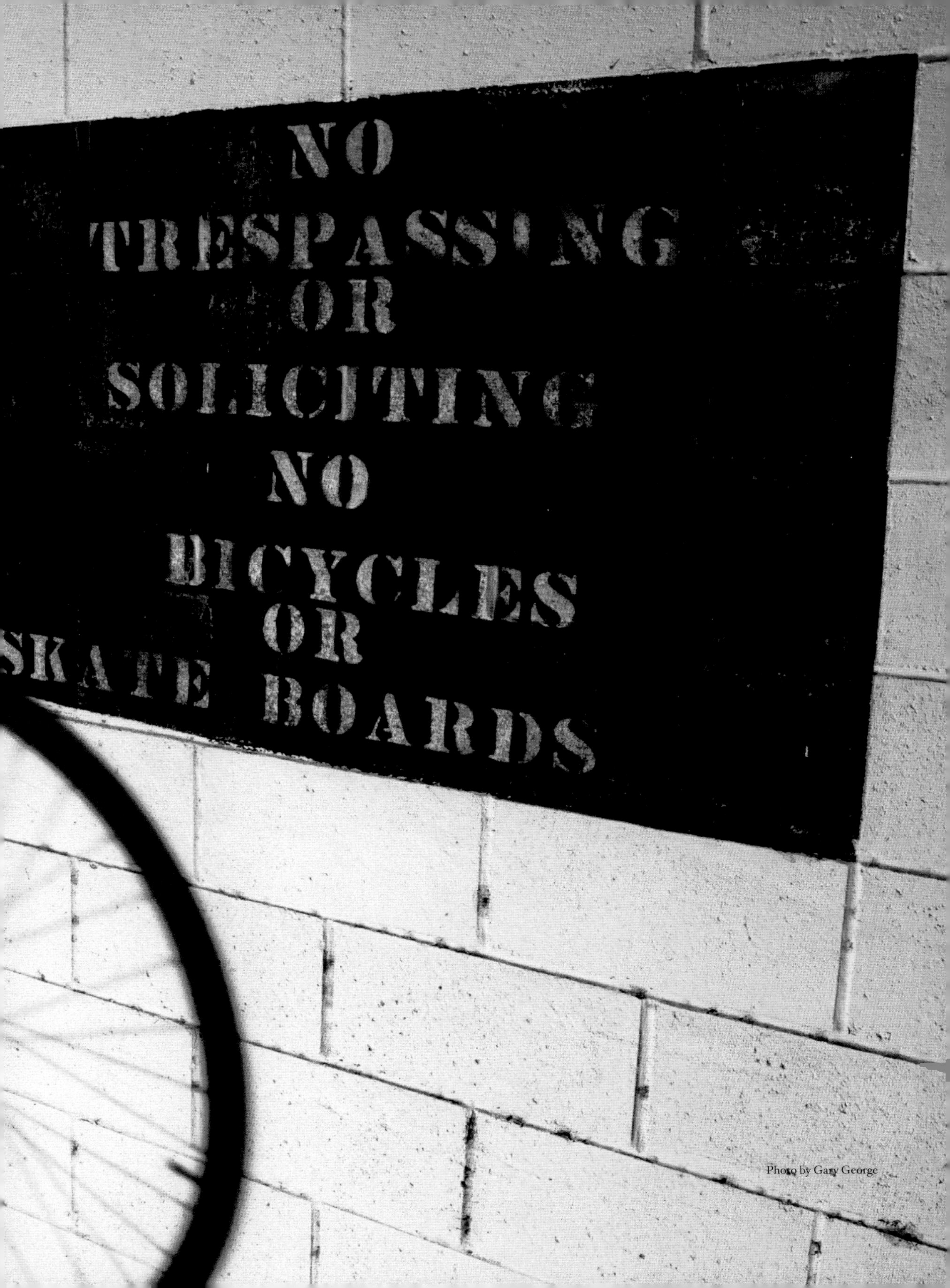
NO
TRESPASSING
OR
SOLICITING
NO
BICYCLES
OR
SKATE BOARDS

Photo by Gary George

Reassembly

This is the final part of the conversion process. Remember when Anakin Skywalker is "born again" as Darth Vader? In EXACTLY the same way, your old road bike will entirely lose its innocence, and be transformed into a slick ride. If you have followed all the steps correctly, and have all the tools ready, the reassembly of your bike will be an interesting and very satisfying task. The process will require a variegated patchwork of techniques, tips and tricks. If you are taking on your first conversion, it's easy to underestimate small details, or think that the order of things can be changed without any consequences. But don't you believe it. In a way, this is rocket science. And, as you'll soon discover, riding a bike that you put together with your own hands is a different experience all together. More often than not, a millimeter will make the difference between a nicely working bicycle and an improperly assembled one.

In this chapter we also explore the various rear drivetrain possibilities in the realm of single-speed bikes, from the straightforward perspective of the purist to hybrid technologies. How you choose which way to go will depend on your budget but also on your personal riding style. So, ladies and gentlemen, prepare your wrenches.

Polafixie, Gaëtan Rossier
www.gaetanrossier.ch

Starting out

After cleaning and restoring your frame, reassembly can begin. Be sure to use padding on the parts that are going to touch the ground or the bike stand, in order not to ruin the new paint job.

Bottom bracket

You should begin by reassembling the bottom bracket. It helps to lay out all the required pieces before proceeding.

From left to right:
1. **Adjustable Cup** *2.* **Bearings**
3. **Lockring** *4.* **Spindle**
5. **Bearings** *6.* **Fixed Cup**

🐇 *At the starting line*, Dave Alexander

Fixed cup *(.6)*

 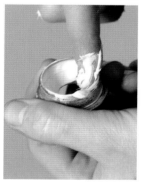

Before reinstalling the fixed cup, you should make sure that it shows no sign of excessive usage. Pits, dents and scratches might seem negligible, but they make for a less smooth ride and quickly and unnecessarily increase wear on parts. Grease has the double function of preventing rust and making the rotation smoother. It's impossible to over-grease the cups, so load 'em up!

Bearings *(.5)*

Insert the bearings into the cup, making sure they're correct side up. Most bikes will have "caged" bearings; these are easier to install and replace, but provide a lower quality rotation than loose balls.

 x11
x2

If you need to replace bearings, it's best to use eleven 0.635 cm loose balls for each cup.

Threading the fixed cup

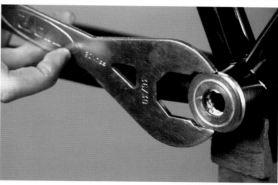

First off, the fixed cup is threaded fingertight on the right, or drive-side of the bottom bracket.

The correct tool is needed to lock the fixed cup in place very tightly. This tool will also give you the correct leverage to set the adjustment at the right tightness.

Fixiehands, Mark Skull
www.markskulls.com

Flipping the spindle

For chainline reasons, it's best to have the chainring as close as possible to the dent in the framestays, anywhere between 4 - 6 mm. This can be achieved by flipping the spindle and installing the shorter side on the drive side.

It's smart to have a dry-run before greasing the parts.

If, after flipping the spindle, the chain ring still doesn't end up at the desired distance from the frame, it might be worth checking different length spindles.

Make sure you check with your local bike shop before buying a new one, as they will usually have a lot of used ones.

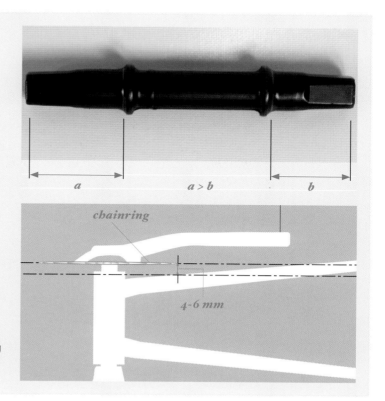

a

$a > b$

b

chainring

4-6 mm

Inserting the spindle (.4)

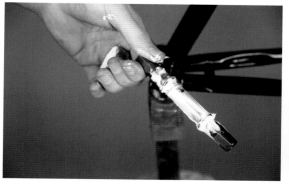

Adjustable cup bearings (.3)

Once the fixed cup is in place, the spindle can be inserted, but remember to smear some grease on it, too.

Clean, inspect and grease the adjustable cup exactly as you did for the fixed cup, and you're ready for reassembly.

Photo by Reggie Biala

Threading the adjustable cup (.2)

Lockring (.1)

The adjustable cup can now be threaded into the other side of the frame.

This component is never meant to be too tight. It's made to be adjusted to just the right distance. Overtightening might compromise the bottom bracket threads or bearings.

The last piece to go on is the lockring. It's better not to thread it too tight, otherwise later fine tuning adjustments you'll need to make will be impossible.

Adjusting the bottom bracket

You should end with no play in the spindle, and it should rotate as smoothly as possible. This is a tricky process, and there are various ways to approach it. This process always involves a little trial and error.

There are two possible cases:
a) The cup tends to turn with the lock ring, and bearing adjustment will become tighter when the lock ring is tightened securely.
b) Tightening the lock ring pulls the adjustable cup out very slightly. With a little bit of practice you'll be able to tighten the adjustable cup correctly, just enough to counteract the loosening action of the lock ring.

Cranks

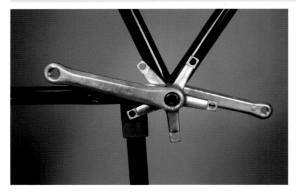

The spindle is made of steel and the cranks are made of aluminum. The taper fit is ensured by inserting the cranks very tightly.

⚓ If there is even a tiny bit of space left over, the rotation of the steel spindle will deform the aluminum.

Three-piece cranks usually have screw-on, nutted type spindles, which will enable you to apply the correct torque to the crank bolts.

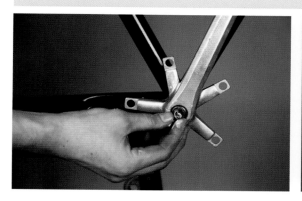

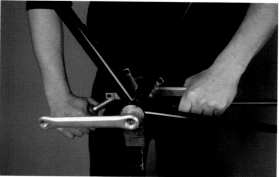

Greasing the ends of the spindle isn't recommended; nevertheless, it's a good idea to smear a bit of grease on the threads of the nuts and the back where it touches the crank.

The reverse of the crank puller will have a socket into which the crank bolts fit perfectly, allowing you to tighten them.

Drivetrain

When the cranks are in place, it's time for the chainring and matching bolts.

🔖 Most roadbikes will mount a 39 and a 52 tooth chainring. A gear ratio of 5-6 is optimal for city riding. Thus, you should mount either a 13t or a 16t sprocket on your rear wheel, depending on which chainring you choose up front.

Mounting the chainring

The first step is to place the chainring on the crank correctly, aligning the bolts with the spider.

Holding the crank still, insert the bolts and tighten them with your fingers.

Chainring bolts

A quick and easy fix is to stack washers under each nut to make up the required thickness.

After tightening, the chainring should be perfectly attached to the spider, with no movement whatsoever.

Photo by Damiano Merlo

Chainring bolts

One of the most common problems at this point, is that the chainring bolts are probably too long to clamp the chainring to the spider. This is due to the fact that they were made to keep two chainrings in place.

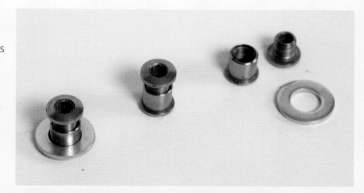

Of course, you can buy shorter chainring bolts, but it's usually possible to adapt the old ones using one of the following methods.

a) If you have access to a vise, it's easy to clamp the bolts down and shorten them with a file.
b) With 3-chainring sets, the bolts will probably have to be shortened with a hacksaw.
c) If it's only small difference to make-up, washers are an easy fix.

Photo by Damiano Merlo

How to use a caliper

It is essential to use a caliper when determining chainline. It's impossible to be as precise if you rely on a simple ruler.

1. Outside jaws: mainly used to measure the external width of an object.

2. Inside jaws: useful to measure internal widths, such as the inside a tube.

3. Depth probe: can be used in tight places or narrow holes

4. Main scale: with a precision of a tenth of a mm.

5. Main scale: gives measurements in fractions of inches.

6. Vernier: with a precision of a hundredth of a cm.

7. Vernier gives measurements in fractions (of inches)

8. Grip

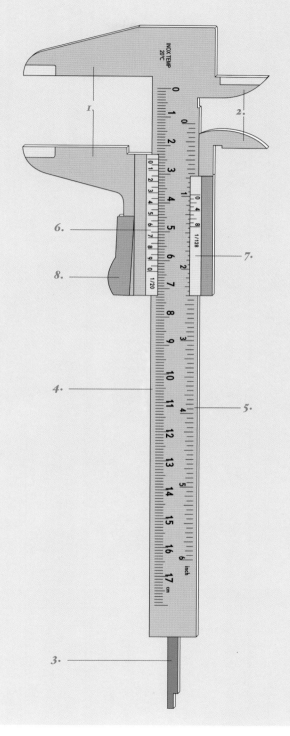

Determining chainline

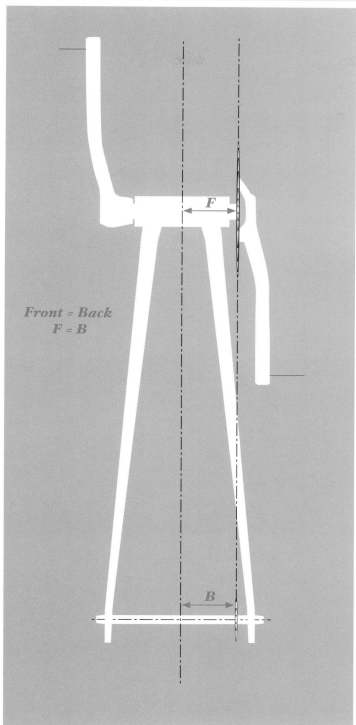

Front = Back
F = B

Photo by Damiano Merlo

The term chainline refers to how straight the chain runs between the front and rear sprockets.

On a fixed gear bike, it is possible to place both the chainring and the cog on the same plane, in order to avoid sideward motion and stress to the chain.

This is what is known as "perfect chainline".

$F = B$.

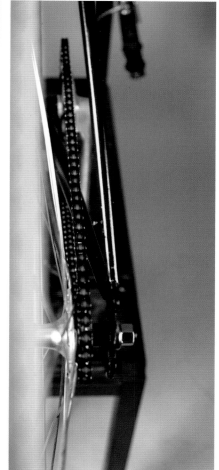

Front chainline

Chainline is measured from the centerline of the frame to the center of the chain.

The **first step** is to measure the diameter of the down tube. We'll refer to this measurement as F_1.

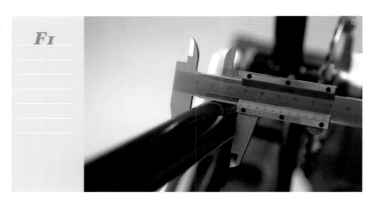

The next measurement is from the outside of the seat tube to the center of the chainring teeth. F_2

This is not a chainline measurement because it's not from the center of the tube. But all you have to do is use simple math and subtract half of the seat tube width from this measurement.

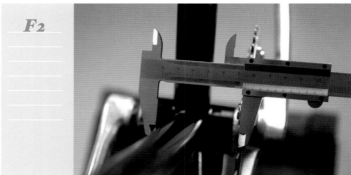

Back spacing

The **next measurement** to take is the rear, or 'frame', spacing'.

Place the caliper from the inside of the fork ends (drop outs), exactly where the locknuts would rest. B_1

On older bikes, the dropouts might be a bit spread out, coming together when the bolts are tightened. For this reason, it's best to measure the hub too.

The spacing of a hub is measured from the outside of the cone locknuts, where they touch the frame's fork ends.

There is a mnemonic for the spacing dimension: *OLD* (Over-Lock-nut Distance).

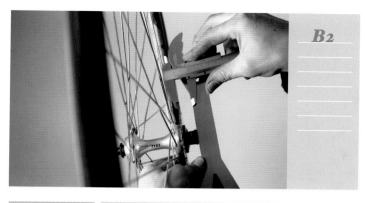

B_2

Back chainline

For measurement purposes, the fixed sprocket is threaded on. The back chainline is measured from the center of the sprocket teeth to the outside face of the locknut. B_2
In order to take a precise measurement, one trick is to place a wrench or any other straight bar on the edge of the outside face of the locknut and measure to that.

F

B

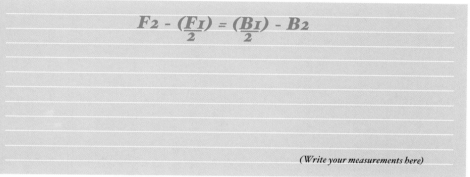

$$F_2 - \frac{(F_1)}{2} = \frac{(B_1)}{2} - B_2$$

(Write your measurements here)

Now, this simple equation will enable you to calculate chainline.

Once you have determined Front and Back chainlines, you will need to equalize the two numbers, i.e. bring the front chainring and the back sprocket onto the same plane. There are a number of ways of doing this:

Front: The easiest thing is to flip the spindle, to gain (or lose) a few millimeters. There are also spacer washers between the right-side bottom bracket mounting ring (or cup) and the bottom bracket shell of the frame. Another option is to add spacers between the chainring and the crank spider.

Back: Most likely, you'll need to gain millimeters on the back chainline: this is done by way of adding spacers behind the outer locknuts, between the locknuts and the cones.

Redishing the wheel

If your back wheel held a multiple gear sprocket freewheel or cassette, the spokes were dished to center the wheel accounting for the extra space needed on the drivetrain side. When you get rid of all that extra space by adjusting the axle to compensate for reduced back chainline, you will also have to redish the wheel. This is done by moving the rim to the left, centering it again at the center of the frame.

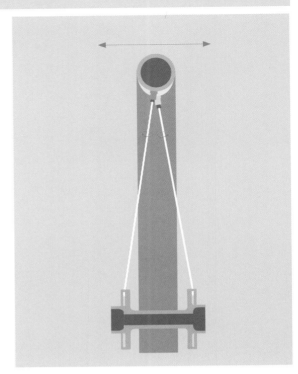

This can be done directly on the bike without the need of a bike stand. Anything that can give you a reference, like clipping a piece of paper to the chain or seat stays will help you determine which way the rim is moving.
Before you do anything, loosen the spokes and lubricate them.
The spokes and nipples are basically a nut and bolt pair, with the spoke being the bolt and the nipple being the nut. Their adjustment determines tension on each side.

The spokes hold the rim exactly where it needs to be. If all the spokes ran right into the middle, however, the wheel would lack side-to-side strength. For this reason, the spokes reach the flanges on each side of the hub. They also determine where the rim is in relation to the hub.
When the spokes end up tighter on one side than the other, the rim is going to be "pulled" towards the side with higher tension.
Your job here is to reduce the tension on the side closest to the spokes, while increasing it on the opposite side. This is done by tightening and loosening the spokes with the appropriate spoke wrench.

It is very important to use the correct size wrench in order not to damage the nipples.

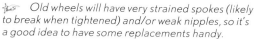

🖝 Old wheels will have very strained spokes (likely to break when tightened) and/or weak nipples, so it's a good idea to have some replacements handy.

🖝 Be sure to apply spray lubricant to rim eyelets and spoke threads, so they'll be easier to thread.

🖝 Don't try to move the rim just by tightening or loosening spokes on just one side of the hubs. You're likely to pull the rim out of true.

🖝 When using the wrench, make sure you're only turning the nipple, and not "winding up" the entire spoke..

Start at the tube valve hole and proceed to loosen the right side spokes half a turn. Don't overdo it! Spokes are under very high tension and even small adjustments count. This adjustment will have already begun to move the rim to the left. The loosening on the right side will increase the tension on the left side by itself. Spoke tension won't be sufficient, however, and you will have to compensate for that by tightening the left side spokes.

Continue this process until the rim is centered in the frame. It'll probably take two or three rounds to get it right, depending on how far you need to move the rim.

If the rim needs further adjusting, it's better to repeat the process as a whole instead of turning the spokes more than half a turn at a time. This way you won't risk throwing the wheel out of true.

Riding on water by Andy Miller

Rebuilding the headset

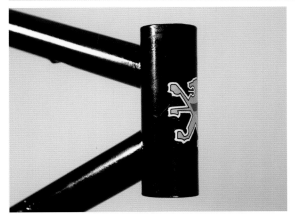

The first thing to do when approaching a headset reassembly is to make sure all the pieces are properly cleaned and clear of pits. It helps to line them up and have them ready.

Installing top and bottom headraces

The part of the frame where the fork will be housed (the head tube) has to be inspected for rusty residue and grime.

🖛 The interior of the head tube doesn't touch any of the moving parts but eventually that grime will end up in the bearings, so it's a good idea to clean it on the inside.

Headraces are taper fit, so they must be pressed in.

🖛 When dealing with older bikes with steel frames and steel cups, it's ok to hammer them in (with the rubber side!).

Crown race

Next is the bottom crown race. This piece will be in contact with the bearings so it must be carefully inspected for pits and dents before installation.

It must be fitted onto the fork very snugly. A copper tube is the perfect cheap tool to use as it is softer than the steel and it should not damage the headset. Plastic, or PVC pipe also works in a pinch.

Using a hammer, strike the top of the of the copper tool until the race is fully seated. It's important to listen carefully, as the sound will change as it seats.

📌 Make sure not to leave a gap between the fork and the bottom crown race.

📌 If you are dealing with an aluminum frame and pricier headraces, it's best to go to your local bike shop and get them pressed in with a special press.

Both headraces have to be thoroughly greased. Both will house the bearings, and are fine-tuned, moving parts.

Tattoo Boys by Matt Taylor
www.matttaylor.co.uk

The bottom crown race should be greased too.

Place the bottom bearings over the bottom crown race.

Once the bearing is in place, it's a simple matter of inserting the steering tube into the frame, and then slipping the top bearing into the top headrace.

🐟 The bearings have a top and a bottom. Check for the open side of the ball retaining cage.

The open side should face the bottom crown race (or the top cup). Before greasing, install everything for a test fit to make sure it runs properly.

🐟 If the cage is in the right position, it will run smoothly. Otherwise the cage retainer will rub against the race, increasing friction. Reverse the cage and test again.

Tattoo boys Matt Taylor
www.matttaylor.co.uk

The rest of the headset reassembly is very straightforward–if you have followed the steps correctly, that is, and the pieces were all properly aligned as recommended at the beginning of the section.

Simply thread on the adjustable top race.

...then the washer....

...and the fork cone locknut.

🐟 The fine tuning of the headset is a delicate process, and it's easier to complete these final adjustments at a at a later stage. So the locknut should also be fitted finger tight until the wheel is in place.

Stem installation

Most old bikes have traditional expander or wedge quill stems.

Vintage road bikes use threaded forks, and have a stem that slides into the fork's steering column. The stem will have a long bolt running down through the vertical part, connecting to a wedge at the bottom. Tightening the bolt pulls the wedge up, jamming it against the inside of the steerer, securing the stem to the steering column.

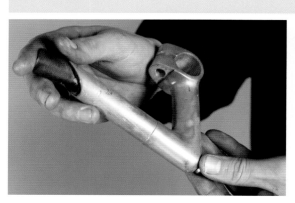

Start by inserting the bolt into the stem and threading it just enough to secure the wedge.

The stem will have to be inserted into the fork tube so it's a good idea to apply some grease to prevent rust. A brush is useful to spread grease evenly on the stem, on the wedge and inside the fork tube.

Stem adjustment

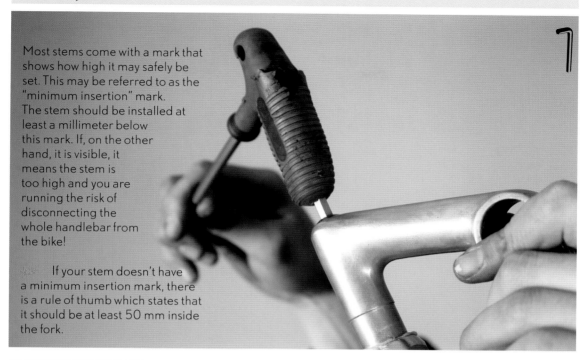

Most stems come with a mark that shows how high it may safely be set. This may be referred to as the "minimum insertion" mark. The stem should be installed at least a millimeter below this mark. If, on the other hand, it is visible, it means the stem is too high and you are running the risk of disconnecting the whole handlebar from the bike!

☞ If your stem doesn't have a minimum insertion mark, there is a rule of thumb which states that it should be at least 50 mm inside the fork.

Handlebar

Most racing bikes come with a "Mæs" bend handlebar. This is a tubular handlebar in which the highest point is at the middle. Drop down horns are used to switch riding positions, which is essential for continuous comfort on long rides.

After cleaning the handlebars of any residual tape glue or grease, insert them through the stem. They are usually kept in place by a nut and bolt, and their assembly is pretty straightforward.

☞ If it looks like the stem opening could scratch or damage the handlebar, be sure to use a very fine file to reduce the burrs.

Tires by Jason Rosete

Installing and replacing tires

The vast majority of bikes use standard clincher tires. These tires are also known as "wire-on." The outer tire is u-shaped and an inner tube contains the air. Thick edges, or beads, "clinch" under the rim while under air pressure, holding the tire in place. There are three structural components of a clincher tire: Bead, Fabric and the Rubber.

Bead

Beads are found on the lowest part of the u-shaped cross section of the tire. They are made of twisted steel threads and are essential structural components of the tire. Some higher-end tires use Kevlar® in their beads to increase flexibility and save weight.

Fabric

This is the component that determines the shape of the tire. Cloth fabric is found between the two beads to form the body or "carcass" of the tire. Apart from older tires which will still have cotton and/or silk, 90% of modern tires use nylon cord or similar synthetic fabric threads.
For maximum strength, the cords are laid out in layers (plies) of parallel threads. Each layer is then arranged at right angles on top of the previous one. Thread thickness determines the number of (thread) ends per inch (EPI). This indicates the quality and overall performance of a tire.

Higher end tires have higher EPI (or TPI) numbers and are consequently lighter and roll better. Unfortunately they are also very delicate and can pick up a puncture relatively easily. The arrangement of the plies also affects tire performance. There are two types, depending on the angle at which threads run across from bead to bead. In Bias tires, the plies run on a 45-degree angle to the center of the tire, causing the plies to crisscross.
This results in construction that is less flexible and has shorter tread life.
In radial construction, the plies, or layers, of a radial tire run on a 90-degree angle to the center of the tire. This causes the plies to overlap, resulting in more flexibility and longer tread life. Radial tires were offered on some bikes in the mid 80s but were soon abandoned because they tend to lack side strength, giving the feeling of an underinflated tire.

Some bicycle tires also have a strip of Kevlar ® or other material running under the tread (a sub-tread), in addition to the normal bias plies. This gives added strength and puncture resistance.

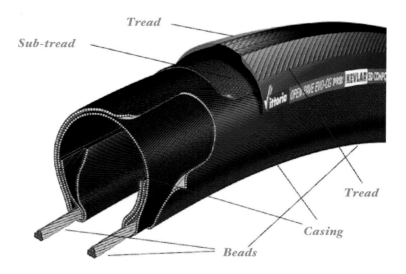

Tread

Sub-tread

Tread

Casing

Beads

Rubber

Contrary to popular belief, the rubber outside has traction and protective functions, but no structural influence on the tire. Rubber coating adapts to the cloth and bead framework, coating it in different thicknesses. The top part of the cross section is where rubber is thickest, mainly for resistance to wear and to prevent puncture. This element of the tire is commonly referred to as 'the tread', and can come in different pattern forms. Road traction is dictated more by different additives to the rubber tread compound than tread shape. Generally, a softer tread compound will give better traction, but will wear more rapidly as a result.

Tire pressure

Opinions differ when it comes to tire pressure, but the bottom line is that there is no "standard" setting. Rider weight, terrain type, and tube and tire types all come into play, and expert riders will experiment with different pressures. The recommended pressure listed on the tire sidewall is a good starting point.

When to replace tires

Tires should be replaced when treads are worn thin, especially as the fabric starts to show through the rubber. At this point, you run the risk of road hazards punching through the tread and reaching the tube. Also, if the tire's fabric has been damaged, the tire won't have the strength to keep its shape, and the tube will deform it.

Side, by Phil Thomas

Rim tape

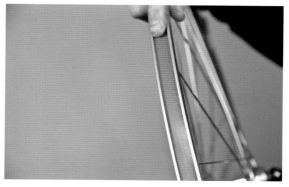

The rim tape protects the tube from mechanical damage from spoke ends, metal burrs and holes in the rim.

An appropriate rim tape must cover all spoke holes completely and securely.

🐟 There are many kinds of rim tape, so be sure to choose one with the appropriate width.

Place the rim inside the first tire bead.

🐟 *Fixie Pier*, by Phil Thomas

Inner tube installation

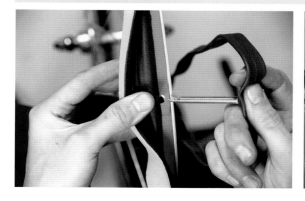

Inflate the tube slightly, until it is round and easier to place evenly into the tire. The first tire bead should fit easily onto the rim.

Carefully fit the valve through the hole and put the cap in place to keep it from falling out again.

Place the tube inside the tire, starting at the valve stem. Work your way around the rim, pushing the tube in with your fingers. Make sure no part of the tube is hanging out or caught between rim and bead.

Tattoo girls Matt Taylor
www.matttaylor.co.uk

The outer bead is harder to install, although on most tires it can be done by hand. Starting again at the valve, work the bead onto the rim using both thumbs.

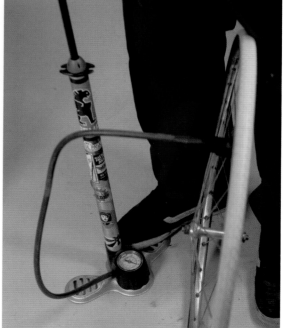

Very tight tires can be helped in with a tire lever. Never use a screwdriver or a similar object, as you risk puncturing the inner tube or tire.

The last step is to inflate the tire to the desired pressure.

Tattoo girls Matt Taylor
www.matttaylor.co.uk

Mounting the front wheel

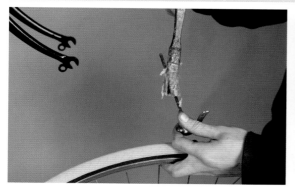

Installing the front wheel is a pretty straightforward process: there will be either two acorn nuts or a quick release axle with a skewer. In the first case these nuts will have to be properly tightened.

In the case of quick-release skewers there are one or two things to bear in mind.

It's good general practice to position the skewer lever on the left side.

Adjust the right side acorn nut as tightly as possible, while still allowing the skewer to close all the way.

Be sure to close the lever running parallel to the fork, as this will help in closing it, and will prevent the lever from catching on anything.

Make sure you grease the spindle and lubricate the quick-release levers before reinstalling the skewers, and don't forget to install the springs pointing inward.

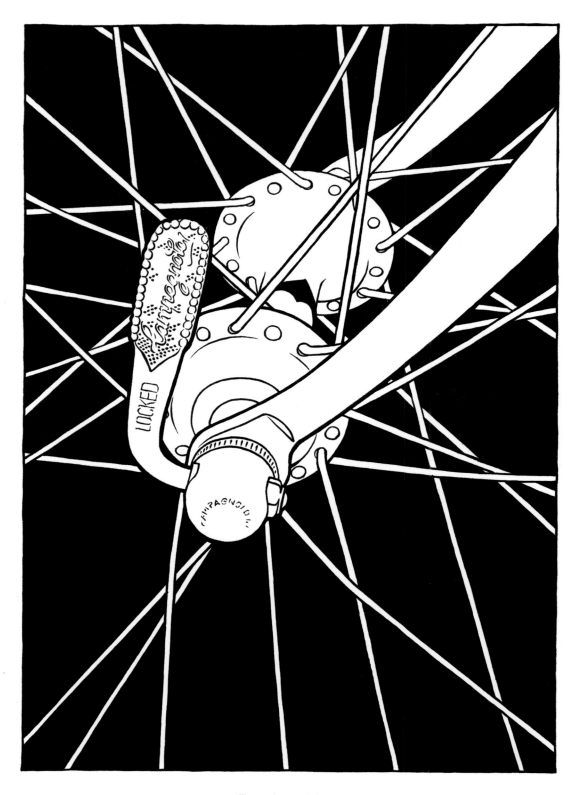

Illustration by Bruno Gallegher

Campagnolo
The evolution of a myth

Back in 1927, during the ascent of the Croce d'Aune–a particularly steep alpine pass, Tullio Campagnolo had great difficulty trying to remove his rear wheel. He immediately recognized the great advantages that a rider would enjoy with a better system, and two years later the quick-release skewer was patented.

In 1933 he founded Campagnolo with the goal of making products for racers by racers.

Tullio Campagnolo was a man of innovation and he soon developed new ideas, literally reinventing the wheel. Following World War II, many of the world's best cyclists–including Fausto Coppi aka "Il Campionissimo" (the super-champion) and Gino Bartali–began using Campagnolo equipment. Campagnolo's emergence as the definitive

component manufacturer was due in large part to the man himself, and to his concept of linking the producer and the end user.
Foreshadowing the R&D of today's companies, Tullio began following the races personally, listening to the suggestions of the riders and modifying the products to meet their needs.

Today Campagnolo components and especially vintage track sets are rare merchandise and go for very high prices on eBay or dedicated bike sites.

Tullio himself with an old rod-shifter bike.

Headset fine tuning and troubleshooting

The headset and its bearings allow the fork to turn smoothly while in motion. Pitting and dents in the cups are a very serious matter, as they lead to problems such as poor steering, indexed steering (brinelling), and rapid part wear.

Worn out headsets tend to "lock up" when the front wheel is pointing straight. This happens when pits are so deep that bearings get stuck in them.

Another common problem derives from poor adjustment. The two sets of races that enclose the bearings are designed to be adjustable to just the right tightness by way of an adjustable top race and locknut. If this is threaded too tightly there will be binding, and if too loosely there will be an annoying play between the parts. This causes the bearing parts to knock together, wearing them prematurely.

Once you have installed handlebar, front wheel and brake, it's easy to test and "diagnose" for both of these problems. To assess an indexed steering tube, gently swing the handlebars back and forth from center. Pitting in the cups will cause the headset to stick as it passes through center position. A pitted headset should be replaced.

To test for play, place the bike on the ground and grab the front brake tightly. Press downward on the handlebars and rock the bike back and forth. A knocking sensation may indicate a loose headset. In effect, this does the same thing as grabbing and pulling on the fork. However, play in the brake caliper arms may also cause knocking. If you suspect that bearing surfaces may be worn out, or the ball bearing retainers may be upside down, or a seal may be improperly aligned you should disassemble headset and start over. If play always seems present no matter the adjustment, the threaded steering column may be too long for the locknut. Add headset washers under the locknut in this case. If this is not the problem, cups may be loose in their press fit in the frame. If everything is moving smoothly after these two tests, you can proceed to tightly threading the locknut, thus completing headset assembly.

Installing handlebar tape

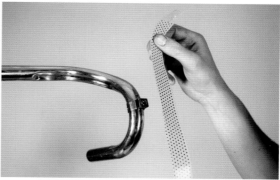

Wrapping handlebar-tape takes skill and patience. You might need a few tries before you get it right, so it's a good idea to do a dry-run first: wrap the tape around without removing the seal; you'll get an idea of how much you have to overlap it. The idea is to wrap it evenly, leaving it as clean and as comfortable as possible.

The first thing to do is install the brackets that will hold the brake levers in place, as these will be surrounded by tape.

☞   Start at the top of the bar. Cut the tape at a sharp angle. This will help you roll the tape in a more uniform manner.

The direction of the wrap is important as it may affect the rider's ability to grip the handlebar firmly. When moving from the top part of the bar, one tends to pull the handlebar, rolling the tape inwards.

Wrapping in one direction or the other will either make the tape looser or tighter with time, so you should choose according to how you want your handlebar tape tightness to evolve.

Wrapping

Handlebar tape is not all the same. Different brands vary in length and strength. Test the tape by pulling it very tight and getting familiar with its breaking point.

Assume the roll won't be too long, and use less overlapping in the low section and more on the top part of the bar, which is likely to see more use.

Most of the time, wrapping will involve trial and error, often moving forward and then backing up. Be especially careful at the bends and around the brake socket. The tape must pass the brake levers and wrap tightly around the socket, adding one or two wraps past it.

Make sure you'll have enough tape to fit both sides of the handlebar, as this will enable you to finish up neatly when you install the caps. If you're unsure of the tape's total length, then minimize the overlap..

Finishing touches

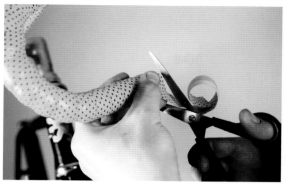  

Roll the tape two more wrap lengths and use scissors to cut the tape cleanly. If the tape isn't completely straight on top of the bar, use a sharp knife or razor blade to make a cut in the tape.

Take care not to make any incision marks, thus ruining the handlebar.

Use your piece of PVC or electrician's tape to end the wrap. Wrap the tape neatly, taking care to maintain a clean and narrow wrap.

Take the slack left over and push it into the handlebar. It will fold inside leaving no gaps between the end of the bar and the plug.

Brake levers

At this point you can install the brake lever. Tighten the inside screw to secure the lever to the socket. Make sure it fits snugly onto the handlebar.

After making sure you have the end of the right wire, pull the brake and weave it inside.

The next steps in installing the brakes are described in *Front brake installation overview.*

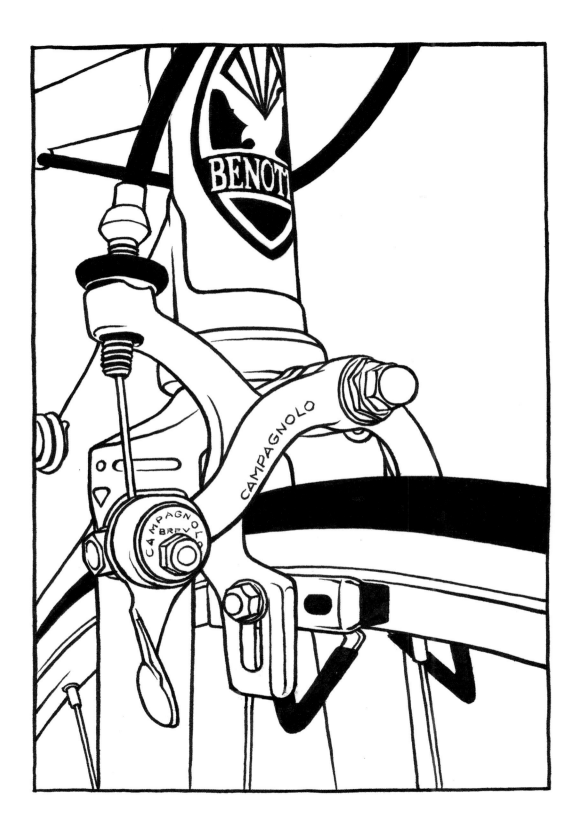

Front brake installation overview

Most older road bikes use caliper brakes (as do most bikes, in fact).

These brakes use an inward-moving mechanism to push the brake shoes onto the rim, thereby causing friction and effectively causing the bike to slow down. Both caliper arms rotate on a single pivot, centered over the wheel.

Front caliper brakes are installed on the bike by means of a pivot bolt through the center of the fork crown, with a seating pad adapted to the roundness of the tube.

Brake systems are usually adjusted very precisely. Installation is relatively straightforward but adjustment is always a question of attention to small details.

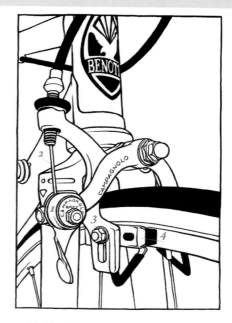

1. **Cable clamp nut** *2.* **Brake cable** *3.* **Brake shoe bolt** *4.* **Brake shoe**

After cleaning the brake and lubricating the center pivot, install the brake by threading the nut, bolt and corresponding washer.

The brake should be as centered as possible with respect to the wheel. Don't tighten it too much as it will need to be rotated before the final adjustment.

Brake pads (or brake shoes) have a threaded stay that allows them to be installed on the brake by tightening its corresponding nut and washer.

Illustration by Bruno Gallagher

Installing brakepads

As the pads wear thinner, they will tend to strike higher on the rim's braking surface, so they'll have to be positioned further down to brake effectively.

Brake pads are crucial for safety, so it's highly recommended to replace them when they show signs of wear.

Samurai, by 中村和人

Cables

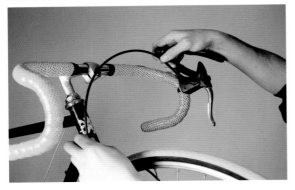 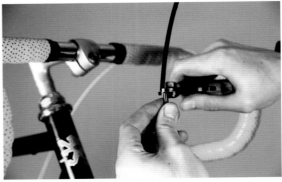

Modern bike cables are composed of an inner and outer part. The inner wire is made of twisted strands of steel. The outer casing is also steel, but it is coiled so as to surround the wire.

This design ensures a good resistance to compression, and avoids extreme bending and consequent malfunction of the wire.

Cable housing might appear to be made of plastic, but it's actually steel. The outside is a plastic covering to protect it from moisture. Without this plastic, the steel would also damage and rust the frame.

Before installing the front brake cable, the first thing to do is measure the proper length.

 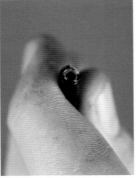 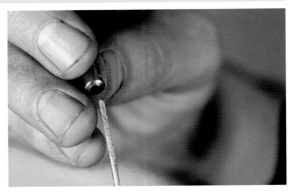

It's important that the handlebars have enough play to turn in both directions without being limited by the cable length. Spiral cable housing shouldn't be forced to bend too much.
The length of the cable shouldn't interfere with the brake levers. Bends should be as gradual and as short as possible, as recommended above.

Be careful when cutting the cable housing. It's important that your clippers get in between the wire instead of mashing the coil flat. This tends to create burrs that hinder wire movement.

Once you have cut one end to the desired length, start inserting the brake cable from the lever to the caliper by the factory end.

To grease or not to grease

Many manufacturers advise against the use of grease, as it can impair wire movement. Clearly, it should be avoided if you happen to employ sealed-systems. Although modern (i.e. post 1970's) cable housing has made greasing the cable unnecessary, there are still some cases in which it is appropriate to apply grease.

Some handlebar/brake lever configurations will force tight bends with sharp angles. In this situation, it helps to grease.

In addition, bikes which will be used or stored in wet or humid conditions may benefit from lubrication or greasing as a way to deter rust.

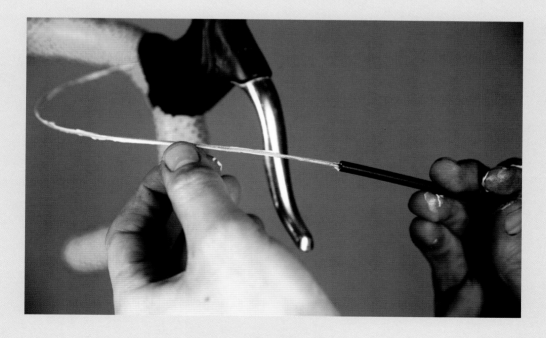

Insert the wire from the lever into the adjustable sleeve, continuing through to the anchor bolt. Thread the barrel adjuster all the way down.

Many road brake systems have a quick release mechanism that loosens the brake enough that you can remove the wheels. If this is the case, make sure it's at the tightest setting, with the brakepads as close as possible to the rim.

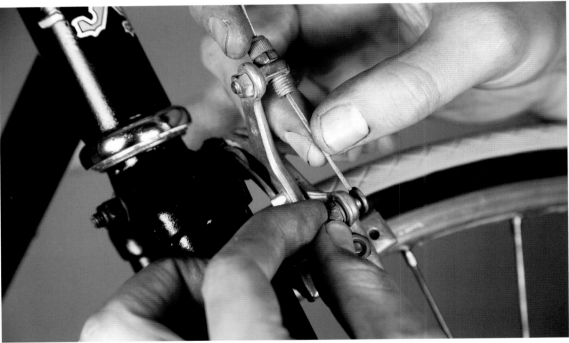

Both adjustments should be finger tight, but do use a wrench if you can't make the anchor bolt hold the wire by tightening with your fingers alone.

Brake shoes are next. Start by positioning them at the appropriate height so they strike the center of the rim sidewall.

🔖 Make sure both left and right brake pads rest at the same height.

Some newer brakes might feature a yaw angle (toe-in), so that the front of the brake pad touches the rim before the back. To avoid squealing noises, the rear of the pad should have a 1-2mm gap when the front first contacts the rim.

Adjust cable tension by loosening the anchor bolt just enough to pull the wire. The fourthand is very useful here, as it allows you to maintain tension on the wire while tightening the anchor bolt.

The next step is to adjust the main center bolt. It is correctly adjusted when the brake functions easily without binding. Check that the brake is centered. Both pads should touch the rim at the same time. Adjustment is

made by loosening the main back bolt and using a wrench to keep the thick washer on the other side still. Center the brakes with the wrench and then tighten the bolt.

A very thin centering wrench is needed, but a pedal or cone wrench will sometimes do.

🔖 This procedure involves trial-and-error, as the brake will move while you're tightening.

Set in motion part IV, by Dave Alexander

Brake fine adjustment

The last step is to tighten the brake pads in their optimal position.

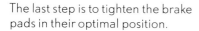 At this point it's also a good idea to lubricate the central pivot with a drop of oil or spray on grease, but take care not to get any lubricant on the brake pads or braking surface of the rim.

Excess wire can be cut with a cable cutter. Be sure to leave 10-20mm of wire for fine tuning adjustments in the future.

Cable end

To ensure that the wire doesn't unravel, install an aluminum cap and clamp it on the wire with your pliers..

Credits:

1. Bryan Smith
2. 中村和人
3-6-7. Chris Willmore
4. Brad Serls
5. BartoszJanczak
8. Annamarie Cabarloc
9. Alex Pink
10. Will Manville

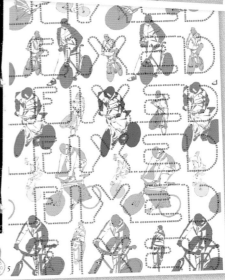

Wheelbuilding

by *Roger Musson* author of
Professional Guide to Wheelbuilding
available at www.wheelpro.co.uk

The assumption here is that wheels need truing on a regular basis and this is generally not the case since a well-built wheel is very reliable and you can expect many trouble free miles from it. However things can go wrong, especially with old bikes. The initial build may not have been too good or a spoke may have broken and any of these situations can leave you with an out of true wheel. Intermittent rubbing on the brake pads is the obvious indicator that the wheel is out of true. This is important even for bikes that don't use brakes, because an out of true wheel is a sign that something is not right and needs fixing before it develops into something more serious.

The advantage of learning some basic wheel maintenance techniques, means there's no need to take your bike to a shop and it takes your self-reliance one stage further—perhaps the final stage in being totally independent.

To fix an out of true wheel the only bike-specific tool you require is a spoke wrench. Recommended brands are Spokey, which fits all European spoke nipples, Park Tool also manufactures very reliable tools. A dedicated truing stand isn't necessary neither for wheel fixing nor for building one from scratch. It's possible to use the bike frame and fork to hold the wheels whilst truing.

I'll now describe how to true a wheel, try and understand the logic so you can adapt the techniques to other situations you may encounter but if it's out of true due to a crash or large impact that results in a bent rim then the following will not apply and you need to learn how to replace a rim.

1) Spin the wheel and see where the rim touches the brake pad (or some reference temporarily taped to the frame). If it touches then it needs pulling away and this is accomplished by tightening a spoke on the opposite side.

Don't try to achieve the same result by loosening a spoke on the side where it touches the brake pad! The overall true might be fixed, but the spoke tension will be compromised.

2) In the out of true region look for a spoke that has lost some tension: this is done by plucking the spokes on the opposite side like a guitar string. The low tension culprit will soon appear (and it's usually a matter of one) emitting a duller tone compared to the neighboring spokes.

Mark it with a piece of tape in order to recognize it easily. This is important because you may over tighten it and cause an out of true in the opposite direction in which case you need to slacken this same spoke, you could even turn the wrench in the wrong direction making the out of true much worse, so knowing which spoke is being adjusted helps a lot.

The tape will also tell you if the spoke is twisting rather than tightening, if it twists (i.e. the tape rotates) more than 180 degrees it's likely the spoke nipple is seized so there's not much you can do and you'll have replace the spoke. In most cases, it will twist 90 degrees or less before starting to tighten. After the initial spoke twist has stopped, tighten in 1/4 turn increments or less for fine truing to avoid the rim from moving.

If the wheel was true except for a localized gap at the brake pads then the rim will need to be pulled towards the pad by tightening a spoke on the pad side.

🐟 It's a very logical process so it's best to never make a guess because the odds are stacked against you, think twice and adjust once!

Replacing a broken spoke follows a similar procedure. You'll need to purchase one of the correct length then it's just a matter of loosely putting it through the hub and into the rim. It can only go in one way and you'll have the other spokes in the wheel to guide you. Don't be concerned about putting a few bends in it, that's inevitable and won't cause any problems, just straighten it a little before attaching the nipple. Prior to tensioning you must put some oil onto the spoke threads and into the rim where the nipple sits.

In a well-built wheel all the spokes on each side of the wheel should have uniform tension and this is the number one requirement in a reliable wheel and a good indication of the skill of the original builder. If you find yourself continually having to true your wheels and you notice that the spoke tensions (by plucking spokes and checking the tone) have substantial variation then the wheel will require more work, namely balancing the tensions and stressing the wheel. The conceptual step from these more basic skills to building a new wheel from scratch isn't so difficult to take, and the tools needed are very few. A dish gauge can be replaced with a profiled piece of cardboard with a measuring reference in the center. The truing stand can be home made from wood, and an old screw driver can be converted into a nipple driver. Mastering these skills will get you far, from replacing a worn out rim—spokes can be used over and over again—building any wheel components you want. You'll always be riding on the very best wheels possible!

Wheel, Cog, by Gaëtan Rossier
www.trucnul.net

Sprockets, Torpedoes®, Archers, lock rings, whips and glue.

A single-speed bike is ultimately about simplicity. Fixed-gear users prefer a more intimate rapport with their bikes, whilst free-wheel riders enjoy an arguably safer ride with reduced strain to knees and muscles. Then there are the in-betweens. Popular coaster brake hubs allow you to coast but stop the bike when you back pedal. Different products offer quick fixed-freewheel alternation (flip-flop hubs, SRAM Torpedoes) or add gearing systems like Sturmey-Archer hubs. Whichever way you decide to go depends on your budget, typical riding environment and general style.

There are essentially two ways to convert your bike to fixed gear:
installing a new fixed hub or modifying the existing hub.

The first is the soundest and the safest way. Track (or fixed) hubs have a double thread. The main thread is the same as in a freewheel hub, but outside of this there is a left (reverse) threading of a smaller-diameter section.
No matter how hard the sprocket is used while braking it will never unscrew. There are many options out there, ranging from cheap to very expensive, and quality varies accordingly.

If your idea is to keep your existing rear wheel, there are several ways to go. If you have a modern Shimano® cassette hub, it can be fixed using a Surly Fixxer® or other similar product. In case you have an older, right threaded hub, installing a fixed sprocket can be risky as backward pedaling tends to unscrew it.

There are many ways to try to lock the sprocket without a lockring, but none of them are 100% safe, mechanically speaking. To secure the sprocket, people have been known to use glue, liquid steel, and other inventive solutions. We describe the Pettenella Method, attributed to Italian track legend Mario Pettenella.

Smashing by Karl Addison
www.idrawalot.com

Securing a fixed sprocket without a lockring (Pettenella's method)

Thread the sprocket onto the rear hub by hand and tighten. With the chain resting on the bottom bracket shell and on the rear sprocket, place the rear wheel in the dropouts.

Make sure the wheel is secured on dropouts, and wrap the chain around the sprocket.

Pull the chain and wrap it around the sprocket as tightly as you can.

At this point it should be straight around the bottom bracket shell and tight around the fixed sprocket.

Hold the the rim of the wheel firmly and rotate in an anti-clockwise direction. Don't overdo it or you may damage hub threads.

The increased leverage of the rim applies a much greater tightening torque than just using a chain whip.

Installing a new wheel

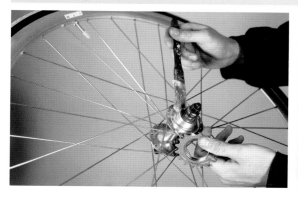 

It's a good idea to apply some grease to the threading to ease tightening and prevent rust.

Next, use the chain whip tool and turn clockwise to tighten the cog.

Black and white fixie, by Gaëtan Rossier
www.gaetanrossier.ch

Henry Ho from Stockton, Ca. at a
Sjfixed alley cat and trick comp event
photo by Annamarie Cabarloc
www.iminusd.com

Sprocket & lockring

Once the sprocket has been properly tightened, install the lockring on the reverse threads.

Tighten the lockring using a lockring tool. You can use the one designed for the lockring on the adjustable cup.

Girl bike by Martin Jones aka Martipans

Installing the chain

You will have to size up your chain before installation. The quickest way is to place the rear wheel in the middle of the dropouts and determine the number of chain links to get rid of.

After determining chain length, install the chain using a chain tool and then pull the wheel to achieve desired chain tension.

Tensioning the chain

Chain tension on a single speed bike is fundamental, and even more so if it is a fixed-gear. A good rule is that the chain should be as tight as possible without binding or skipping.

On the other hand the chain must never be too loose, or else you risk it falling off.

Tightening the rear wheel

To determine the correct tension, pedal the bike. With the chain in motion, push it towards the wheel.

The chain shouldn't fall or rattle excessively. If the chain comes off, move the back wheel further back on the dropouts.

 When you have achieved correct tension, it's time to tighten the axle nuts.

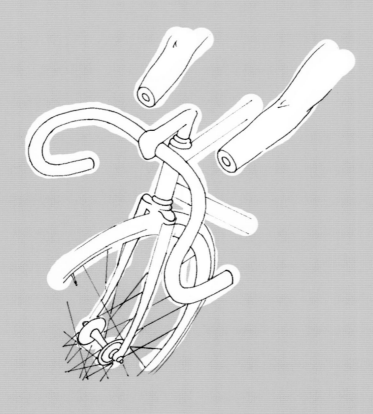

LOOK
MA!
NO
HANDS

Locking your seat in style

Getting your bike seat stolen is no fun, but fortunately there's an easy, cheap and stylish way to lock it.

After you've set the seat at your right height, get an old piece of chain and cut it to the desired length, so it will circle around the wheelstays and the seat.

Inner tube recycling

The old chain is pretty ugly by itself, but not if you slide it inside an old inner tube.

When you're sure of all the measurements close the chain using the chaintool.

Thieves F*@# off!!

By tying the inner tube with a knot under the seat everything will be nice and tight and the bike seat will be safe!

Look Ma! No Hands, by Carlito Schilirò

Tina Tru aka Tinaballs at a photo shoot for
Urban Velo photo by Annamarie Cabarloc
www.iminusd.com

Installing pedals

Install the new pedal with a pedal wrench, or with a normal 15mm wrench if your crank allows you enough space.

Toeclips have a strap to adapt them to your foot. Slide each strap in the front of the pedal as shown.

Next, bolt the plastic toeclips to the pedals and slide the strap through the toeclip tops, and then into the buckle where you'll adjust the fit to your riding comfort.

Threading options

If you are converting an older French or Spanish bike, especially low-end ones with cotter cranks, be careful as they might not have standard threading

Standard 3-piece cranks:
14.28 x 1.27 mm
9/16" (0.56") x 20 tpi

Old French/Spanish:
14 mm x 1.25 mm
0.55" 20.32 tpi

Finito!

Your converted bike is now ready for a test drive!

Take it easy on the first run. Try the brakes, the steering, and the pedals. A final check of the front and back wheel nuts is recommended after your first test ride. Ride safely!

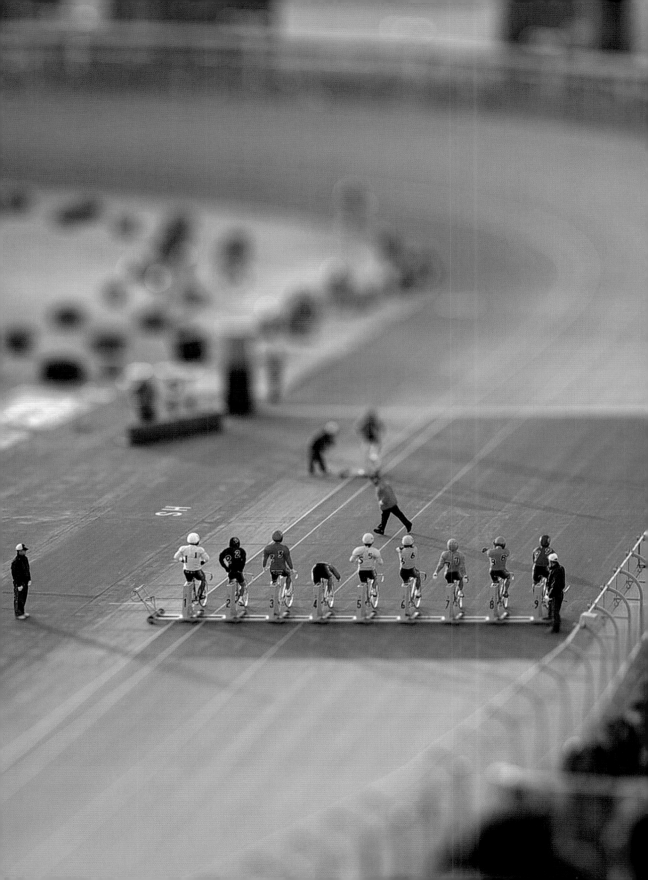

Keirin, by 中村和人

One less car by Lucie Kim & Felix von der Weppen
www.myorangebox.com

> *"Every time I see an adult on a bicycle, I no longer despair for the future of the human race."*
>
> H.G. Wells

Conclusion

The verb "to live" can have many meanings. Living can mean simply being alive, or it can mean, living it up! Just like "to live", the verb "to ride" will assume different meanings for different people.

Throughout the years bikes have meant many things for many people, from a simple commuter vehichle to a collector's item. For aficionados, there has always been unquestionable passion for the object itself and attention to every minute detail.

We hope you will enjoy the sheer freedom and ease that a fixed-gear or single-speed bike will give you, and the satisfaction that comes from having transformed it from scratch.

Riding, like living, can be simple but it doesn't have to be plain.

Glossary

The right name for the right part

In order to disassemble and reassemble your bike it is necessary to acquire a basic vocabulary of the essential parts of the bike. Proper terms have been used throughout the book: they are all here for consultation.

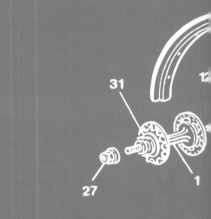

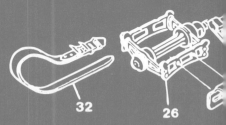

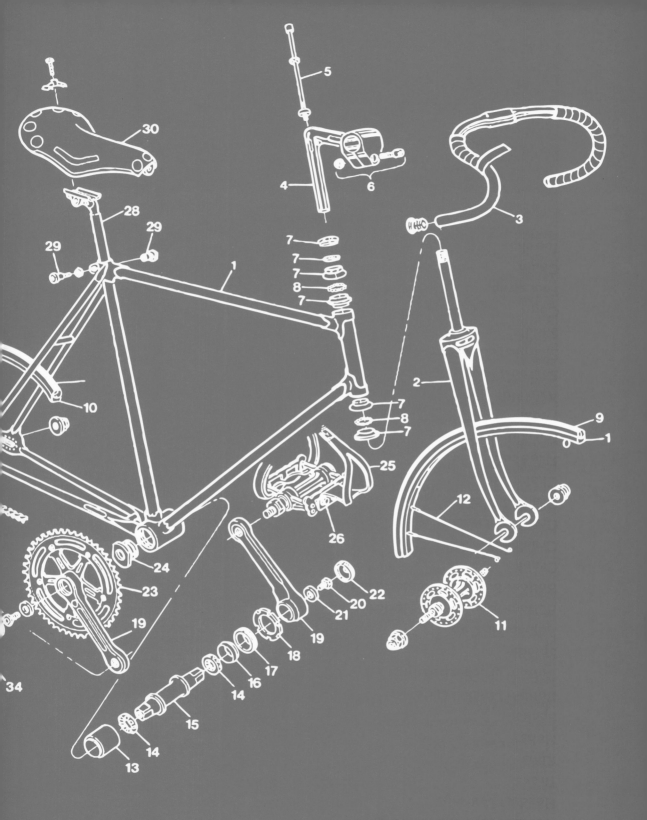

The following people made this book possible:

Luca Gambi, Camilo Diestre Rivera, My Beautiful Parking Barcelona, Joshua Kampa - Arc-En-Ciel Bycicle Studio, Peter Jon White of Peter White Cycles, Roger Musson, Rasmus Folehave Hansen, Hernan Rodrigo Alescio, Rubén Cruz, Stephen Turner, Ivo Gretener.

Thanks to all the collaborators (published or not):

Adam Thrower, Alejandro Carrillo, Alex Pink, Andrey Maximovich, Andy Miller, Angelo Calilap, Annamarie Cabarloc, Bartosz Janczak, Brad Serls, Bruno Gallagher, Bryan Smith, Carlito Schiliró, Carson Ting, Chris Willmore, Christian Webber, Cristian Marin at Enciclika, Domingo Cavenati, Damian King, Damiano Merlo, Dave Alexander, Noor Azlan Mohamed, Edward Pepper, Enrico e Tommaso Bellé, Frank Schott, Gaëtan Rossier, Gary George, Guilherme Caldas at Candyland Comics, Herman Van Hulsteijn, Jake Marx, Jason Rosete, Jesse Brew, Jonathan Winstone, Joseph R. Webb, Kai Streets, Karl Addison, Lucas Prescivalle, Levi Bear, Mark Skulls, Martin Jones, Matthew Hodson, Matt Taylor, Mike Merkenschlager, Matt W. Moore, Olesya Shchukina, Lucie Kim at My ORB, Philip Thomas, Andrea Carlo Gallo at Pollo Design, Rasmus Folehave Hansen at Refurbs, Regidor Biala, Rhys Logan, Samuel Chisholm, Simone Artale, Taylor N. Hurley, Tomas Guidi, Mobius Cycles, Wilis Johnson, Will Manville, 林 辰崎,中村和人.

www.onegearbook.com